IN THE SEA

D1403923

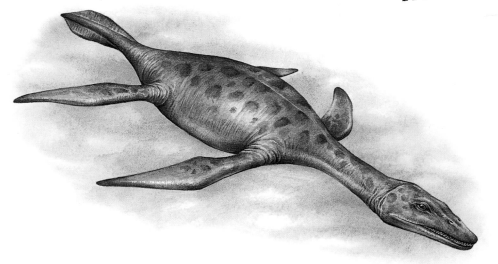

by Dougal Dixon

Gareth Stevens Publishing
A WORLD ALMANAC EDUCATION GROUP COMPANY

CONTENTS

Please visit our web site at:
www.garethstevens.com
For a free color catalog describing Gareth
Stevens' list of high-quality books and
multimedia programs, call 1-800-542-2595
(USA) or 1-800-387-3178 (Canada). Gareth
Stevens Publishing's Fax: (414) 332-3567.

Library of Congress Cataloging-in-Publication Data
available upon request from publisher. Fax (414) 336-0157
for the attention of the Publishing Records Department.

ISBN 0-8368-3329-5

First North American book fair edition published
in 2002, first North American editions published in
2001 as two volumes, *In the Sea* and *In the Sky*, by
Gareth Stevens Publishing
A World Almanac Education Group Company
330 West Olive Street, Suite 100
Milwaukee, WI 53212 USA

U.S. editions © 2001 by Gareth Stevens, Inc. First
published by ticktock Publishing Ltd., Century
Place, Lamberts Road, Tunbridge Wells, Kent TN2
3EH, U.K. Original editions © 2001 by ticktock
Publishing Ltd. Additional end matter © 2001 by
Gareth Stevens, Inc.

Illustrations: John Alston, Lisa Alderson, Simon
Mendez, Bob Nicholls, Luis Rey
Gareth Stevens editor: David K. Wright
Cover design: Katherine A. Goedheer
Consultant: Paul Mayer, Geology Collections
Manager, Milwaukee Public Museum

All rights reserved. No part of this book may
be reproduced, stored in a retrieval system, or
transmitted in any form or by any means,
electronic, mechanical, photocopying, recording,
or otherwise, without the prior written permission
of the copyright holder.

Printed in Hong Kong

1 2 3 4 5 6 7 8 9 06 05 04 03 02

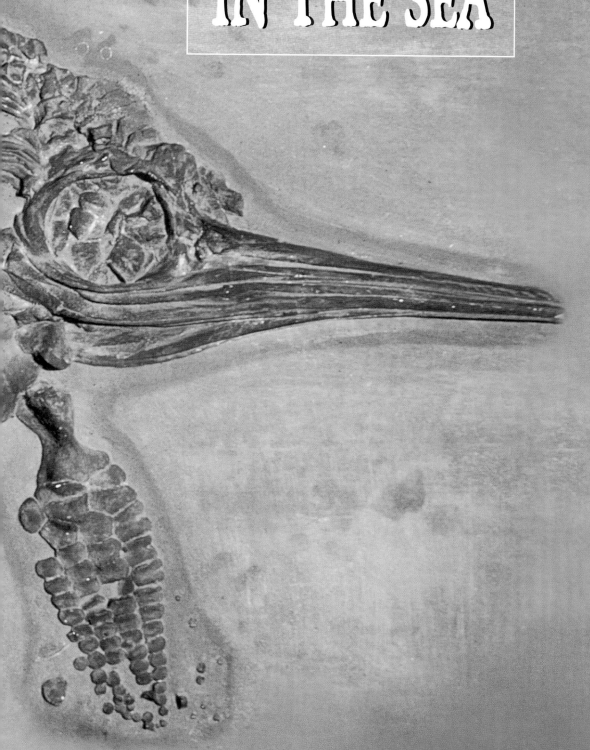

IN THE SEA

A RETRO-PIONEER

Spinoaequalis, the earliest-known land animal to return to a water-living existence, was a lizardlike beast found in Upper Carboniferous marine sediments in Kansas. Its name means "equal spine," which refers to the strong spines on the tail that made a flat vertical paddle to which strong muscles were attached. This is the tail of a swimming animal. The rest of the skeleton is that of a land-living creature.

A FRESHWATER PUZZLE

Mesosaurus was a freshwater reptile, about 3 feet (1 meter) long, with a flattened swimming tail and powerful webbed hind legs. It probably used its tail and hind legs to drive itself through the water and steered and stabilized itself with its webbed front feet. Its teeth were fine and needle-like and were probably used for filtering invertebrates from the water to eat. The odd thing about it, though, is the fact that its skeletons are found in Lower Permian rocks in both South Africa and Brazil. Scientists wondered how the remains of a freshwater animal were fossilized on two widely separated continents. It was the first piece of evidence in support of a revolutionary concept called "plate tectonics."

ABOUT PLATE TECTONICS

In Permian times, when *Mesosaurus* was alive, there was no Atlantic Ocean. What is now Africa and South America were part of a single vast landmass called Pangaea. The same kinds of animals lived all over the world because there were no oceans to separate them. The presence of the skeleton of *Mesosaurus* in South Africa and Brazil was one of the first pieces of evidence supporting the theory of continental drift — now better known as "plate tectonics."

THE FIRST SWIMMERS

All life came from the sea. Scientists estimate that life appeared 3.5 billion years ago and that plants and animals only relatively recently came out on to land (about 400 million years ago for plants and 300 million years ago for animals). Some of the first land creatures evolved into reptiles and dinosaurs. But the ways of evolution are complex. Almost as soon as life on land was established, some life forms returned to the sea to exploit new food sources. As early as 250 million years ago, water-living animals had evidently evolved from land-living ancestors.

A MODERN EXAMPLE

The Galapagos marine iguana, which looks and lives very much like some of the early swimming reptiles, has adopted a partially aquatic way of life because it feeds on seaweed. Its lizard body, legs, and feet show that it is a land-living animal, but its muscular, flexible tail is ideal for swimming. It also can hold its breath for long periods, and it can remove from its system excess salt absorbed from seawater. These are adaptations that fail to show up on fossil animals, so we do not know if early swimming reptiles had them.

THE BUOYANCY PROBLEM

Hovasaurus, from Upper Permian rocks found in Madagascar, had a swimming tail twice the length of its body. Although this tail was so long that it would have been difficult to use on land, its feet were those of a land-living reptile. Most skeletons of *Hovasaurus* have pebbles in the stomach area. Evidently *Hovasaurus* swallowed stones to adjust its buoyancy underwater. This swimming technique was used by animals whose ancestors were land-living animals (*see page 14*).

PERMIAN 354-290 MYA	CARBONIFEROUS 290-248 MYA	TRIASSIC 248-206 MYA	EARLY/MID JURASSIC 206-159 MYA	LATE JURASSIC 159-146 MYA

THE CRETACEOUS SEAS

The shallow seas of the Late Cretaceous (such as those that covered central North America) were filled with ammonites. By this time, the ammonites were not just free-floating and actively hunting ammonites; they also included drifting, filter-feeding forms and crawling types, such as giant snails, that fed on the seabed. The fish-hunters of the shallow waters were the mosasaurs, while out to sea lived the elasmosaurs and the giant pliosaurs. Pterosaurs still fished from the sky, but they were now joined by the creatures that were to be their successors — the birds.

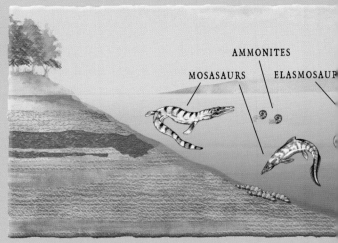

AMMONITES

MOSASAURS   ELASMOSAUR

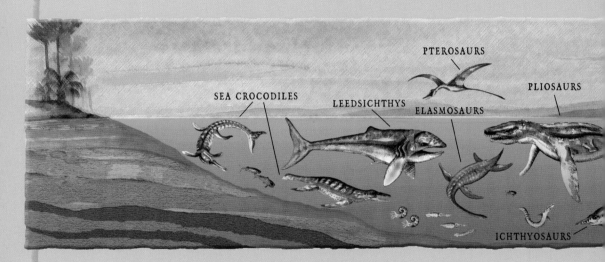

SEA CROCODILES

PTEROSAURS

LEEDSICHTHYS

ELASMOSAURS

PLIOSAURS

ICHTHYOSAURS

THE TRIASSIC SEAS

Shellfish on the shallow floor of the Triassic seas were eaten by slow-moving placodonts. Fish were chased by nothosaurs, which were precursors of the plesiosaurs. Long-bodied ichthyosaurs also chased the fish and ammonites (a prehistoric mollusk) of the time. We are still not sure where the giant ichthyosaurs fit into this pattern. They were probably fish eaters and ammonite eaters as well, and they could hunt in deep water.

ICHTHYOSAURS

PLACODONTS

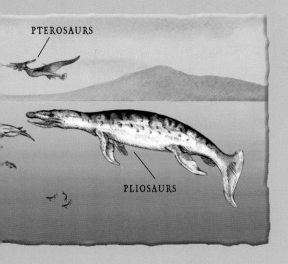

PTEROSAURS

PLIOSAURS

THE JURASSIC SEAS

The shallow seas that covered much of what is today northern Europe were bountiful in Jurassic times, supporting many different kinds of animals. One of these was *Leedsichthys*, a giant filter-feeding fish that must have lived and fed like a modern basking shark. In shallow waters lived sea crocodiles, which fed on the fish of the area. The fish and ammonites of the deeper waters were hunted by ichthyosaurs, while closer to the surface they were hunted by elasmosaurs, which were, in turn, hunted by the great pliosaurs. Dipping into the waves to fish were the flying reptiles, the pterosaurs.

NOTHOSAURS

GIANT ICHTHYOSAURS

AN ECOLOGICAL OVERVIEW

The prehistoric seas and oceans were full of life and supported complex food chains. At the bottom of the food chain were algae, growing and reproducing by absorbing energy from the Sun and taking nutrition from the water. Filter-feeding animals like mollusks fed on these and in turn were preyed upon by fish and other vertebrates. Higher up the chain, these creatures were threatened by even bigger invertebrates that were themselves foodstuff for the largest and most powerful of the sea animals. When any of these animals died, their decaying bodies provided nutrition in the seawater, allowing the algae to grow. The links in this process produced a cycle of life, death, decay, and new life.

LIFE AFTER DEATH

The science of taphonomy deals with what happens to an animal after it dies and how it becomes a fossil. Here is how this process occurs at sea.

1. When an animal dies, it may float on the surface for a while until the gases generated in its decaying tissues disperse.

2. Eventually, it sinks to the bottom of the sea. A less buoyant animal may go straight to the bottom. There it may be scavenged by bottom-living creatures, its parts broken up and dispersed.

3. If sand and mud are being deposited rapidly on the seabed, the body is quickly buried before too much damage is done.

4. After millions of years, the sand and mud will be compressed and cemented together as rock, and the bones of the dead animal will have been replaced by minerals. It will have become a fossil.

A MODERN TURTLE

The turtle is a slow-moving aquatic reptile that is shelled above and below. Its paddle limbs allow it to move through the water with a flying action. Protected from its enemies and surrounded by sources of food, it does not need speed or a streamlined shape to thrive.

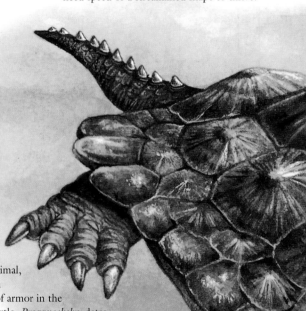

AN EARLY WINNER

A broad body shape works well for a slow-moving animal, but such a creature remains vulnerable to attack from predators. This threat encouraged the development of armor in the reptiles that we know today as turtles. The earliest turtle, *Proganochelys*, dates from the Late Triassic and lived in Germany. Its body shape and the arrangement of its shell are very similar to the modern turtle, which has not changed much in 215 million years.

BIG IS BEAUTIFUL

The biggest turtle known, *Archelon*, cruised the inland sea that covered much of North America in Late Cretaceous times. At almost 13 feet (4 meters) long, it was bigger than a rowboat. Its shell was a system of bony struts covered by tough skin, much like the skin of the biggest of the modern turtles, the leatherback. It probably fed on soft things, such as jellyfish, and like the modern leatherback, its jaws were not very strong.

A SCHOOL OF SWIMMING REPTILES

We have a good record of water-living animals because, in an environment where sediment constantly accumulates, these creatures have a better chance of becoming fossilized. From these fossils, we know that many sea creatures were in fact reptiles that left dry land for a new life in the water. With more food in the water than on land and fewer predators in the sea, an aquatic life would have been appealing. Reptiles can adapt easily to such a lifestyle. They have a low metabolic rate and can cope without oxygen for some time. In addition, moving around in water takes only about a quarter of the energy of moving around on land.

BASILOSAURUS (WHALE)

MOSASAURUS (MOSASAUR)

METRIORHYNCHUS (CROCODILE)

CYMBOSPONDYLUS (ICHTHYOSAUR)

ZYGORHIZA (WHALE)

DOLICHORHYNCHOPS (PLESIOSAUR)

BAPTANODON (ICHTHYOSAUR)

DELPHINOSAURUS (ICHTHYOSAUR)

AN IDEAL SHAPE

The best shape for an underwater hunter is a streamlined body with a strong, flattened tail and paddle limbs. Many of the Permian, Triassic, Jurassic, and Cretaceous swimming reptiles were built like this, as were the Tertiary whales. Some had strange adaptations, such as long necks, that probably enabled them to reach prey hiding in rocks.

TRIASSIC 248-206 MYA	EARLY/MID JURASSIC 206-159 MYA	LATE JURASSIC 159-144 MYA	EARLY CRETACEOUS 144-97 MYA	LATE CRETACEOUS 97-65 MYA

PLACODONTS - THE SHELL SEEKERS

PLACODUS

The most typical of the placodonts was *Placodus* itself. In appearance it looked somewhat like an enormous newt, about 7 feet (2 m) long, with a chunky body, a paddle-shaped tail, webbed feet, and a short head.

Water-living animals may have evolved from land-living animals for a variety of reasons. Most persuasive of these is the idea that when a good food supply exists, nature will develop something to exploit it. Shellfish represent one such food supply. The earliest reptiles that seemed to be well adapted to feeding on shellfish were the placodonts. Although they still needed to come to the surface to breathe, they rooted on the bed of the Tethys Ocean that spread across southern Europe in Triassic times.

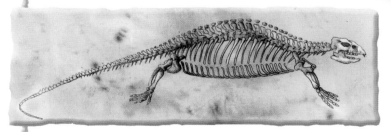

BUILT FOR BUOYANCY

A glimpse of the skeleton of *Placodus* reveals one of its main adaptations to an underwater way of life — "pachystosis." This means that its bones were broad and heavy, perfect for feeding on the bottom of the ocean. Animals that have pachystosis also have big lungs to help regulate buoyancy. To accommodate its huge lungs, *Placodus* developed a broad rib cage. A modern animal with these adaptations is the sea otter. Its weight and large lung capacity enable it to walk along the seabed with ease, hunting shellfish. *Placodus* would have done the same.

TRIASSIC 248-206 MYA	EARLY/MID JURASSIC 206-159 MYA	LATE JURASSIC 159-144 MYA	EARLY CRETACEOUS 144-97 MYA	LATE CRETACEOUS 97-65 MYA

PSEPHODERMA

HENODUS

PLACOCHELYS

MODERN EQUIVALENT

The walrus is a modern sea animal that subsists on shellfish. Its two great tusks are used for prying shellfish from rocks, and it has crushing teeth at the back of its mouth. The tusks are also used as ice picks and for mating displays. We do not know if the protruding teeth of the placodonts had similar functions.

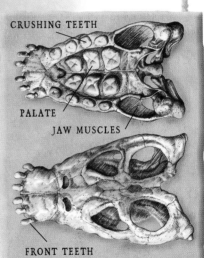

A SHELLED FAMILY

Because they were slow-moving animals, the placodonts must have been vulnerable to the meat eaters of the time. Many developed shells on their backs as protection. In some types, the shells were extensive and looked much like those of turtles, but the two groups of animals were not related. The similar shells developed independently among animals with the same lifestyle in the same environment — a process known as "convergent evolution."

CRUSHING TEETH

PALATE

JAW MUSCLES

FRONT TEETH

POWERFUL BITE

From below, the protruding front teeth of *Placodus* are obvious. These prominent teeth were used for plucking shells from the rocks and the seafloor. Further back, the jaws have strong crushing teeth, and even the palate is paved with broad, flat teeth, all ideal for smashing the shells of shellfish. Holes in the side of the skull show where very powerful jaw muscles were attached. *Placodus* would have eaten brachiopods as well as bivalves similar to those that survive today.

DUCKBILLED PLATYPUS

The duckbilled platypus is a modern animal with many primitive traits, such as webbed feet that push the water back, driving the animal forward. Later marine animals had limbs that evolved into flippers. These flippers were built like wings, allowing the animal to travel through the water using a motion that resembled flying. Nothosaurs seem to represent a stage between the primitive platypus and more advanced sea creatures. Some nothosaurs had webbed feet, while others had paddles.

LARIOSAURUS

NOTHOSAURUS

A VARIETY OF NOTHOSAURS

Although nothosaurs conformed to a particular shape, they displayed much variation within their group. *Nothosaurus* (from which the group gets its name) was 10 feet (3 m) long and had a very long head with jaws full of little teeth. *Lariosaurus*, at 2 feet (60 cm) one of the smallest nothosaurs, was very primitive and looked very much like a land-living animal that happened to be swimming in the sea. Big *Ceresiosaurus*, on the other hand, had feet that were almost like paddles and a small head on a long neck.

TRIASSIC 248-206 MYA	EARLY/MID JURASSIC 206-159 MYA	LATE JURASSIC 159-144 MYA	EARLY CRETACEOUS 144-97 MYA	LATE CRETACEOUS 97-65 MYA

BETWEEN THE LAND & THE SEA

The nothosaurs preceded the plesiosaurs, rulers of the Late Jurassic and Cretaceous seas. Like the placodonts, they are known mostly from sediments laid down in the Tethys Ocean, an ancient ocean that lay between Africa and Europe. Their necks, bodies, and tails were long, and they had webbed feet (although they could walk on land). Their hind limbs were much larger than their front limbs and were used mostly for swimming. They had many small, pointed teeth in long, narrow jaws for catching fish. Nothosaurs seem to represent a stage between land-living animals and fish-eating, seagoing animals like the plesiosaurs.

LET'S GO FISHING

The long jaws and sharp teeth of *Nothosaurus* were ideal for catching fish. The long neck would have been able to reach fast-swimming fish quickly, and the little teeth would have held the slippery prey firmly. These teeth can be seen in such modern fish-eating animals as crocodiles.

CERESIOSAURUS

NOTHOSAUR FOSSIL

Nothosaur fossils have been found in the Alps and in China. Although these animals had legs and toes, their limb bones were not strongly joined to one another and the hips and shoulders were quite weak. This weakened state shows that they were not well adapted to moving on land and were better at swimming than at walking.

STOMACH STONES

Most good fossilized skeletons of pliosaurs contain collections of gastroliths (stomach stones). Sea-living animals swallow stones to help adjust their ballast (weight). For animals that swim fast to catch their prey, this method is a more versatile system than building up the weight of the skeleton through pachystosis, a method adopted by the placodonts (*see page 10*).

PLIOSAUR TOOTH MARKS

The limb bones of an elasmosaur found in Late Jurassic marine rocks in Dorset, England, have given scientists a dramatic clue to the feeding habits of the pliosaurs. Tooth marks punched deep into the bones match the set of teeth of a big pliosaur. Until this discovery, scientists thought that pliosaurs ate only fish and squid.

UNDERWATER ATTACK

From this evidence, we can build up a picture of a Late Jurassic marine incident. A long-necked elasmosaur feeds near the surface. A pliosaur cruises at some depth below, hunting fish and squid. By tasting the water, it knows the elasmosaur is nearby. Vomiting out a few stomach stones, it adjusts its buoyancy to allow it to rise. Then, when its prey is in view, the pliosaur "flies" toward the elasmosaur with strong thrusts of its flippers, closing in on a paddle and ripping it apart with its teeth.

TRIASSIC 248-206 MYA	EARLY/MID JURASSIC 206-159 MYA	LATE JURASSIC 159-144 MYA	EARLY CRETACEOUS 144-97 MYA	LATE CRETACEOUS 97-65 MYA

THE GIANTS OF THE SEA

The plesiosaurs were perhaps the most varied group of swimming reptiles during the time of the dinosaurs. They were ocean-going fish eaters, ranging in size from the length of a small seal to that of a medium-sized whale. They had broad bodies, short tails, and two pairs of winglike paddles with which they "flew" through ocean waters. One group had short necks and long heads; the other had long necks and very small heads (*see pages 16–19*). The short-necked types are called pliosaurs, and the long-necked types are elasmosaurs.

IN FOR THE KILL

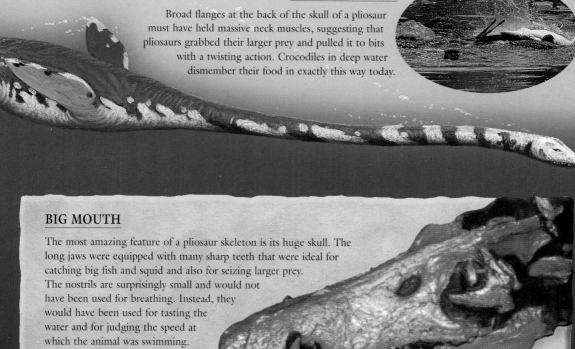

Broad flanges at the back of the skull of a pliosaur must have held massive neck muscles, suggesting that pliosaurs grabbed their larger prey and pulled it to bits with a twisting action. Crocodiles in deep water dismember their food in exactly this way today.

BIG MOUTH

The most amazing feature of a pliosaur skeleton is its huge skull. The long jaws were equipped with many sharp teeth that were ideal for catching big fish and squid and also for seizing larger prey. The nostrils are surprisingly small and would not have been used for breathing. Instead, they would have been used for tasting the water and for judging the speed at which the animal was swimming. A pliosaur probably breathed through its mouth when it came to the surface.

A RANGE OF PLIOSAURS

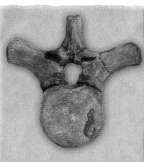

We used to think that pliosaurs were the biggest sea reptiles of all time. Now, however, we are finding the remains of beasts that were even bigger (*see page 25*). Nevertheless, the biggest pliosaurs were very big animals.

Many smaller pliosaurs also cruised the seas. Their different sizes and head shapes reflected their different lifestyles and the different foods they were eating. Some must have lived like penguins, darting and snatching at the weaving and dispersing schools of fish, but the biggest must have been the dolphins and toothed whales of their time. Often, all we know of a particular pliosaur is the skull. Using the skull as a guide and building models based on an agreed-upon plan, scientists have assumed that we can know what the rest of the body was like. Who knows for sure if they are right?

LIOPLEURODON VERTEBRA

This is a vertebra from *Liopleurodon*, which existed in northern European waters at the end of the Jurassic Period. Pliosaurs were a wide-ranging group, with very similar animals existing in Europe at one time and on the other side of the world in Australia 80 million years later. It was probably *Liopleurodon* that attacked the elasmosaur in the incident described on page 14.

MONSTER OF THE DEEP

We used to think that the skull of the pliosaur *Kronosaurus* represented less than a quarter of the length of the whole animal, giving *Kronosaurus* a total length of 40–46 feet (12–14 m) — greater than the contemporary *Tyrannosaurus* on land. More recent studies suggest that the skull was about a third of the total length, making it 26 feet (8 m) long. That's still quite a monster!

TRIASSIC 248-206 MYA	EARLY/MID JURASSIC 206-159 MYA	LATE JURASSIC 159-144 MYA	EARLY CRETACEOUS 144-97 MYA	LATE CRETACEOUS 97-65 MYA

A HALFWAY STAGE

Fossilized bones of sea animals are much more common than those of land animals. They are often found on beaches, where the sea is eroding cliffs made of rock from the Mesozoic Era (which included the Triassic, Jurassic, and Cretaceous periods), or in quarries where rock from the same era is being extracted. One of the most complete plesiosaur skeletons ever found was 16 feet (5 m) long. *Rhomaleosaurus* was uncovered in 1851 from stone quarries in Barrow upon Soar, Leicestershire, central England. It featured widely spread ribs, and it has become the mascot of the village. Scientifically, the odd thing about *Rhomaleosaurus* is the fact that it has a long neck as well as a fairly large head. It is classed as a pliosaur, but it seems to represent a stage between the short-necked pliosaurs and the long-necked elasmosaurs.

SUPER-PENGUINS

Dolichorhynchops was a much smaller pliosaur, about 10 feet (3 m) long. It lived in the seas that covered Late Cretaceous Manitoba in Canada. Judging the animal by its build and its teeth, scientists feel that it swam easily among schools of fish that frequented the waters, snapping them up in its long, narrow jaws. It swam like modern penguins, using paddles to get around.

UNDERWATER FLIGHT

The plesiosaur paddle worked like a wing. Among the pliosaurs, the strongest muscles pushed the paddles forward, providing the animal with its power stroke. Among the elasmosaurs, there was as much muscle to pull the paddle back as to push it forward, allowing the body to turn very quickly and suggesting that the elasmosaurs had much more maneuverability than pliosaurs. Today, penguins use the same kind of swimming action.

"NESSIE"

For hundreds of years, many people have reported sightings of an elasmosaur-like creature in Loch Ness, in the Highlands of Scotland. This convincing picture was taken in 1977. But is it a dinosaur's head or a branch?

ARTISTIC IMPRESSIONS

Because of numerous fossil finds, the remains of plesiosaurs were known to fossil collectors for a long time before dinosaurs were discovered. This 19th-century engraving of a prehistoric coastal scene depicts a giant ichthyosaur being attacked by two long-necked plesiosaurs. Although far from perfect, depictions of sea creatures were much more accurate than those of the land-living dinosaurs from the same period.

ELASMOSAURS - THE LONG NECKS

One early researcher described the long-necked plesiosaurs as "snakes threaded through turtles." The broad body and the winglike flippers are reminiscent of the ocean-going turtle, but the long neck and the little head full of vicious, pointed teeth are very different from those of the placid, grazing, shelled reptile we know today. Elasmosaurs were the sea serpents of their time. They existed alongside the pliosaurs in the oceans of the Jurassic and Cretaceous periods.

FLEXIBILITY

The great length of the elasmosaur neck, with its huge number of vertebrae, has led some to suggest that it would have been as flexible as a snake. But looking at the way the vertebrae are articulated, we can see that this was not quite true. From side to side the neck had a good degree of movement, but the neck was restricted in the up-and-down plane. Although an elasmosaur could reach downward with ease, it could not hold its head up like a swan on the surface.

CRYPTOCLIDUS

Cryptoclidus was a common elasmosaur found in Late Jurassic rocks of Europe. Its mounted skeleton can be seen in several museums. It is typical of the whole elasmosaur group, with its broad body with ribs above and below, the long neck, the mouthful of sharp, outward-pointing teeth, and the paddles made of packed bone.

TRIASSIC 248-206 MYA	EARLY/MID JURASSIC 206-159 MYA	LATE JURASSIC 159-144 MYA	EARLY CRETACEOUS 144-97 MYA	LATE CRETACEOUS 97-65 MYA

ELASMOSAUR LIFESTYLE

Elasmosaurs came in all sizes. As time went by, the group displayed a tendency to develop longer and longer necks. They may have hunted by ambush. The big body was probably used to disturb schools of fish, while the little head at the end of the long neck darted quickly into the group and speared individual fish on the long teeth. Moving the paddles in different directions would have turned the body very quickly in any direction. Their agility meant that elasmosaurs probably hunted on the surface, as opposed to the pliosaurs, who were built for sustained cruising at great depths.

ELASMOSAURUS

We take the name of the elasmosaur group from Late Cretaceous *Elasmosaurus*. This creature had the longest neck, in proportion to the body, of any animal known. It had 71 vertebrae, in contrast to the 28 or so of the earlier elasmosaurs. The neck took up more than half the length of the entire animal.

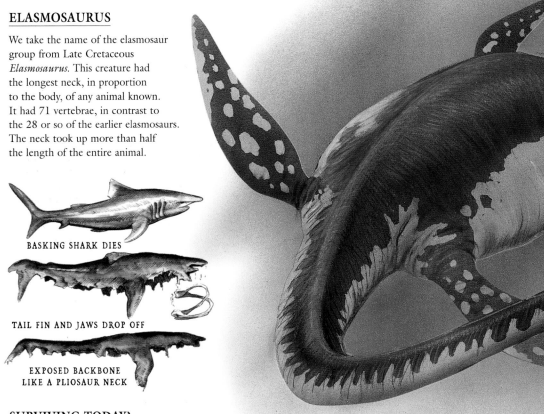

BASKING SHARK DIES

TAIL FIN AND JAWS DROP OFF

EXPOSED BACKBONE
LIKE A PLIOSAUR NECK

SURVIVING TODAY?

Now and then we hear stories of people sighting sea serpents that have a distinct similarity to plesiosaurs. Several photographs exist of rotting carcasses with a plesiosaur look to them. The carcasses usually turn out to be those of basking sharks. Although a basking shark looks nothing like a plesiosaur in life, its dead body deteriorates in a particular pattern. The dorsal fin and the tail fin fall off, losing the shark's distinctive profile. Then the massive jaws drop away. This leaves a tiny brain case at the end of a long string of vertebrae. Instant plesiosaur!

| TRIASSIC 248-206 MYA | EARLY/MID JURASSIC 206-159 MYA | LATE JURASSIC 159-144 MYA | EARLY CRETACEOUS 144-97 MYA | LATE CRETACEOUS 97-65 MYA |

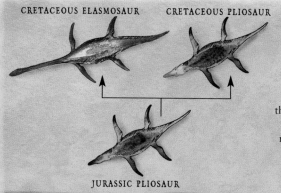

CRETACEOUS ELASMOSAUR   CRETACEOUS PLIOSAUR

JURASSIC PLIOSAUR

THE "POLYPHYLETIC" THEORY

It is possible that elasmosaurs were "polyphyletic," which means they did not evolve from one ancestor. The Jurassic elasmosaurs evolved from the same ancestors as the nothosaurs of the Triassic Period. However, the arrangement of the skull bones of the Cretaceous elasmosaurs has led some scientists to suggest that these later ones actually evolved from the short-necked pliosaurs of the Jurassic Period. The long neck developed independently in response to environmental pressures; there was food to be had for long-necked animals, so long-necked animals evolved. Most scientists, however, believe that all the elasmosaurs evolved from the same ancestors — that is, they were "monophyletic."

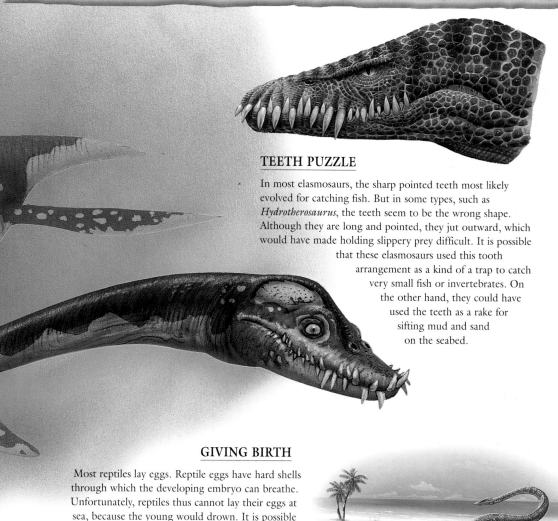

TEETH PUZZLE

In most elasmosaurs, the sharp pointed teeth most likely evolved for catching fish. But in some types, such as *Hydrotherosaurus*, the teeth seem to be the wrong shape. Although they are long and pointed, they jut outward, which would have made holding slippery prey difficult. It is possible that these elasmosaurs used this tooth arrangement as a kind of a trap to catch very small fish or invertebrates. On the other hand, they could have used the teeth as a rake for sifting mud and sand on the seabed.

GIVING BIRTH

Most reptiles lay eggs. Reptile eggs have hard shells through which the developing embryo can breathe. Unfortunately, reptiles thus cannot lay their eggs at sea, because the young would drown. It is possible that elasmosaurs laid eggs the way modern turtles do. This would mean that they came ashore at certain times of the year and scooped out a hole in the beach with their flippers. This process is a great effort for a modern turtle. Just imagine the effort for a 39-foot (12-m) plesiosaur!

A CLEAR IMAGE

Thinly layered, Late-Jurassic rocks at Holzmaden in Germany are so fine that they contain the impressions of the softest organisms that lived and died there. The bottom of the sea (where the rocks formed) was so stagnant that nothing lived — not even the bacteria that normally break down once-living matter. Among the spectacular fossils found there are the ichthyosaurs, with impressions of their soft anatomy still preserved. Flesh and skin still exist as a fine film of the original carbon. With this find, scientists were able to determine for the first time that ichthyosaurs had a dorsal fin and a big, fishlike fin on the tail.

A MODERN RENDERING

Now we can paint an accurate picture of what an ichthyosaur looked like in life. From all the fossils we have found we know that they had streamlined, dolphinlike bodies, with fins on the back and tail. Unlike dolphins, the tail fin was vertical, not horizontal. The ichthyosaur had two pairs of paddles, the front pair usually bigger than the hind pair.

AN ICHTHYOSAUR PIONEER

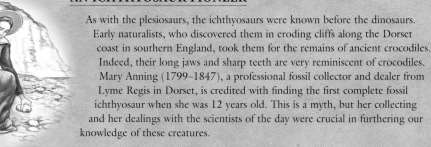

As with the plesiosaurs, the ichthyosaurs were known before the dinosaurs. Early naturalists, who discovered them in eroding cliffs along the Dorset coast in southern England, took them for the remains of ancient crocodiles. Indeed, their long jaws and sharp teeth are very reminiscent of crocodiles. Mary Anning (1799–1847), a professional fossil collector and dealer from Lyme Regis in Dorset, is credited with finding the first complete fossil ichthyosaur when she was 12 years old. This is a myth, but her collecting and her dealings with the scientists of the day were crucial in furthering our knowledge of these creatures.

ICHTHYOSAURS - THE FISH LIZARDS

Without doubt, the most well-adapted marine reptiles of the Mesozoic were the ichthyosaurs. If you saw one swimming, you might mistake it for a dolphin or even a shark. It is all there — the streamlined body, the triangular fin on the back, the big swimming fin on the tail, and the paired swimming organs at the side. Like dolphins, ichthyosaurs were descended from land-living animals and needed to come to the surface to breathe. Although some ichthyosaurs continued into the Late Cretaceous, mosasaurs became the dominant marine reptile during that time (*see pages 28–29*).

ICHTHYOSAUR SKELETON

Entire skeletons of ichthyosaurs are relatively common, since these creatures were frequently fossilized. Many museums have complete ichthyosaur skeletons on display. This ichthyosaur is in the Bristol City Museum in England.

TRIASSIC	EARLY/MID JURASSIC	LATE JURASSIC	EARLY CRETACEOUS	LATE CRETACEOUS
248-206 MYA	206-159 MYA	159-144 MYA	144-97 MYA	97-65 MYA

A RANGE OF ICHTHYOSAURS

Before the standard dolphin shape of the ichthyosaur evolved, this creature came in many different shapes and sizes, particularly among the earlier ichthyosaurs in the Triassic seas. These different types had different lifestyles and swimming techniques. Some were long and narrow like eels, without a significant tail fin. They probably swam with a flying motion, like the plesiosaurs and penguins, and steered with their long tails. Some were the size of whales, with increased bone mass to make them heavier and able to swim in deep water for long periods. This range of Triassic forms soon settled to the classic dolphin shape of the Jurassic ichthyosaur.

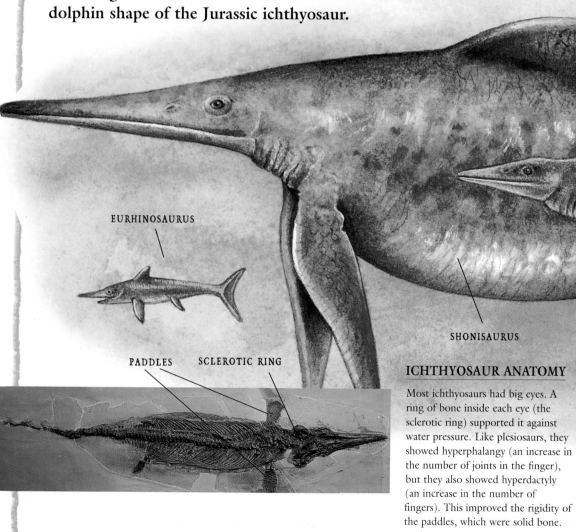

EURHINOSAURUS

SHONISAURUS

PADDLES   SCLEROTIC RING

ICHTHYOSAUR ANATOMY

Most ichthyosaurs had big eyes. A ring of bone inside each eye (the sclerotic ring) supported it against water pressure. Like plesiosaurs, they showed hyperphalangy (an increase in the number of joints in the finger), but they also showed hyperdactyly (an increase in the number of fingers). This improved the rigidity of the paddles, which were solid bone.

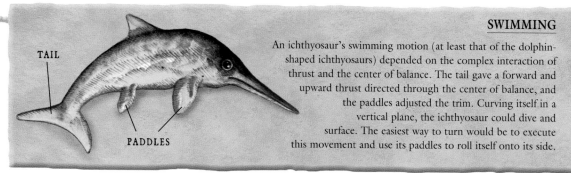

SWIMMING

An ichthyosaur's swimming motion (at least that of the dolphin-shaped ichthyosaurs) depended on the complex interaction of thrust and the center of balance. The tail gave a forward and upward thrust directed through the center of balance, and the paddles adjusted the trim. Curving itself in a vertical plane, the ichthyosaur could dive and surface. The easiest way to turn would be to execute this movement and use its paddles to roll itself onto its side.

TAIL

PADDLES

TRIASSIC GIANT

A truly enormous Triassic ichthyosaur was discovered in British Columbia, Canada, in 1998. At 75 feet (23 m), it was longer than a sperm whale and approached the length of most blue whales. The skeleton is 30 percent longer than any other marine reptile so far discovered, and its head is 19 feet (5.8 m) long. It is being studied and does not yet have a name.

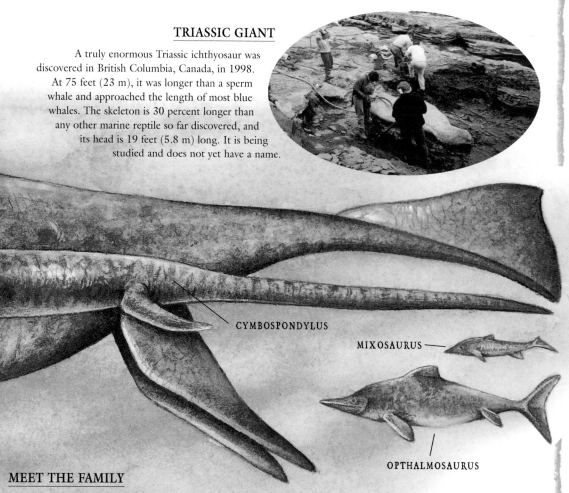

CYMBOSPONDYLUS

MIXOSAURUS

OPTHALMOSAURUS

MEET THE FAMILY

Probably the most primitive-looking ichthyosaur was *Cymbospondylus*, found in the Middle Triassic rocks of Nevada. Measuring 33 feet (10 m), it was a big animal, but its body was long and eel-like. *Mixosaurus*, found in Middle Triassic rocks from around the world, was still long and slim, but it showed the beginnings of the typical ichthyosaur tail. The 49-foot (15-m) monster *Shonisaurus*, from the late Triassic rocks of Nevada, was the biggest ichthyosaur known before the discovery of the Canadian giant *(see above)*. *Opthalmosaurus* was probably the most fishlike and had no teeth in its jaws. It may have fed on soft-bodied animals like squid. *Eurhinosaurus* had a swordfish-like beak on its upper jaw. It possibly used this beak for stunning fish prey.

TRIASSIC 248-206 MYA	EARLY/MID JURASSIC 206-159 MYA	LATE JURASSIC 159-144 MYA	EARLY CRETACEOUS 144-97 MYA	LATE CRETACEOUS 97-65 MYA

ICHTHYOSAURS - DISPELLING A MYTH

The fact that reptiles lay eggs on land is what distinguishes them from their ancestors, the amphibians. Occasionally, however, reptiles that live in harsh environments in which exposed eggs would be vulnerable tend to give birth to live young. Most of the modern reptiles that live in northern Europe, such as the common lizard, the slow worm, and the adder, bear live young. The ichthyosaurs also did this.

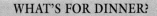

WHAT'S FOR DINNER?

The fossils of baby ichthyosaurs found inside the skeletons of adults once led people to think that ichthyosaurs were cannibalistic. Now we know that this could not have been so, since the young were located a long way from the stomach area. The little skeletons were complete and not chewed up, and they were facing forward, not backward as they would have been if they had been swallowed.

HOLZMADEN

In Late Jurassic times, a shallow sea with scattered islands covered most of northern Europe. To the north was low-lying land, and to the south, beyond a series of massive reefs formed by corals and sponges, lay the open ocean. The region of Holzmaden may have been a seasonal gathering place where ichthyosaurs came to give birth. We can tell much about the ichthyosaurs' anatomy and lifestyle from fossils found in the region. A large number of ichthyosaur remains shows baby ichthyosaurs emerging from the adult. These remains tell us that ichthyosaur birth was a very traumatic event that sometimes proved fatal for the mother.

| TRIASSIC 248-206 MYA | EARLY/MID JURASSIC 206-159 MYA | LATE JURASSIC 159-144 MYA | EARLY CRETACEOUS 144-97 MYA | LATE CRETACEOUS 97-65 MYA |

LITTLE ONES

This ichthyosaur from Holzmaden in Germany has been preserved with the broken-up skeletons of three unborn young still intact. A fourth may just have been born. Its skeleton can be seen below the tail of the parent. The mother must have died while giving birth underwater.

TAIL

BABY ICHTHYOSAURS

FISH FOOD

Belemnites were squidlike animals that swarmed in the warm shallow seas of the Jurassic Period. Like squid, they had tentacles that were armed with tiny hooks, but unlike squid, their bodies were stiffened with bullet-shaped internal shells. These shells are commonly found as fossils in Jurassic rocks. We know that many ichthyosaurs ate belemnites, because we have found masses of their indigestible hooks in the stomach areas of ichthyosaur fossils.

A SWIMMING LIZARD

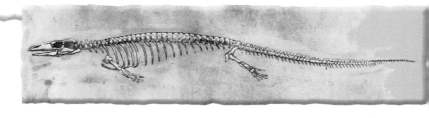

The aigalosaurs were ancestors of the mosasaurs. They were a group of swimming lizards that lived in Europe during the Late Jurassic and Early to Middle Cretaceous periods. They grew to 3 feet (1 m) long and had flattened tails but lacked the specialized paddle limbs of their descendants.

DINNER TIME

There is direct evidence that mosasaurs ate the abundant ammonites of the time. The ammonites were relatives of the modern squid and nautilus and displayed coiled shells that are very common as fossils. They lived throughout the Mesozoic in seas all over the world. One ammonite fossil has been found punctured by tooth marks that exactly match those of a small mosasaur. Evidently, the reptile had to bite the ammonite sixteen times before crushing the shell and reaching the animal.

FAMILY MEMBER?

The bones of *Mosasaurus* were very similar to those of the modern monitor lizard. Despite the extinction of individual species, the same lines of animals were continuing to develop into other forms. The concept of evolution that would explain such phenomena had not been developed when *Mosasaurus* was first studied.

GEORGES CUVIER

Baron Georges Cuvier (1769–1832) was impressed by the jawbones of an unknown giant reptile unearthed from underground quarries near the River Meuse. The French anatomist became convinced that there were once animals living on Earth that were completely unlike modern types and that these ancient animals were periodically wiped out by extinction events.

TRIASSIC 248-206 MYA	EARLY/MID JURASSIC 206-159 MYA	LATE JURASSIC 159-144 MYA	EARLY CRETACEOUS 144-97 MYA	LATE CRETACEOUS 97-65 MYA

MOSASAURS

In 1770, workmen in a chalk quarry near Maastricht in Holland uncovered a long-jawed, toothy skull. The owner of the land sued for possession — a circumstance that is all too common in the field of paleontology, even today. In 1794, the French army invaded Holland and, despite the owner's attempt to hide the skull in a cave, seized it and took it back to Paris. There it was studied by the legendary French anatomist Baron Georges Cuvier. By this time it had been identified as the skull of a huge reptile related to the modern monitor lizards. British geologist William Conybeare gave it the name *Mosasaurus* ("lizard from the Meuse").

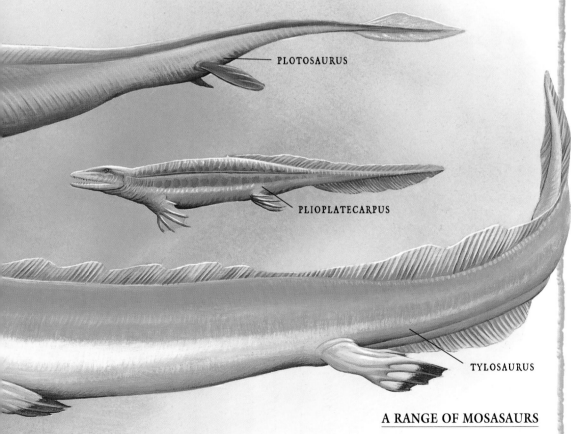

PLOTOSAURUS

PLIOPLATECARPUS

TYLOSAURUS

A RANGE OF MOSASAURS

Mosasaurs are known from Late Cretaceous deposits throughout the world. They were all based on a similar body plan and ranged in size from a few feet to monsters 33 feet (10 m) or more in length. Their heads were all very similar to those of the modern monitor lizard, and their teeth had adapted to snatch at fish or ammonites. An exception was *Globidens*, which had flattened, rounded teeth that were obviously adapted to a shellfish diet.

CROCODILES

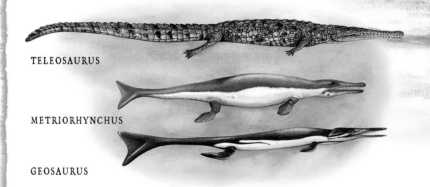

Crocodiles have remained essentially unaltered since Late Triassic times. Throughout their history, however, crocodiles have adapted to many conditions. Some were long-legged and scampered about on land, while some ran on hind legs like little versions of their relatives, the dinosaurs. More significantly, some developed into sea-living forms showing the same adaptations as other sea-living reptiles — the sinuous bodies, the paddle legs, and the finned tails. These features were particularly important in Jurassic times.

TELEOSAURUS

METRIORHYNCHUS

GEOSAURUS

A SELECTION OF SEA CROCS

Teleosaurus was a gharial-like sea crocodile. It was even longer and slimmer in build than *Steneosaurus. Metriorhynchus* was 10 feet (3 m) long and shows much more extreme adaptations to a seagoing way of life. It lacked the armored scales that we see on more conventional crocodiles. Its legs were converted into paddles that would have been almost useless on land. At the end of its tail the vertebral column was turned downward, showing that it had a swimming fin like an ichthyosaur. This was a true sea crocodile. *Geosaurus* had the same adaptations as *Metriorhynchus* but appeared somewhat later and, at 7 feet (2 m) long, was considerably smaller. It was much slimmer, and the jaws were even narrower.

CHAMPSOSAUR

PHYTOSAUR

CROCODILE

A GOOD SHAPE

Many semi-aquatic, meat-eating reptiles have crocodile shapes. The phytosaurs from the Late Triassic could be mistaken for crocodiles except for their nostrils, which were close to the eyes instead of at the tip of the snout. The champsosaurs from the Late Cretaceous of North America were also very crocodile-like, having the same lifestyle in the same habitat. None of these animals was closely related to another. This pattern is an example of "parallel evolution" (*see page 34*).

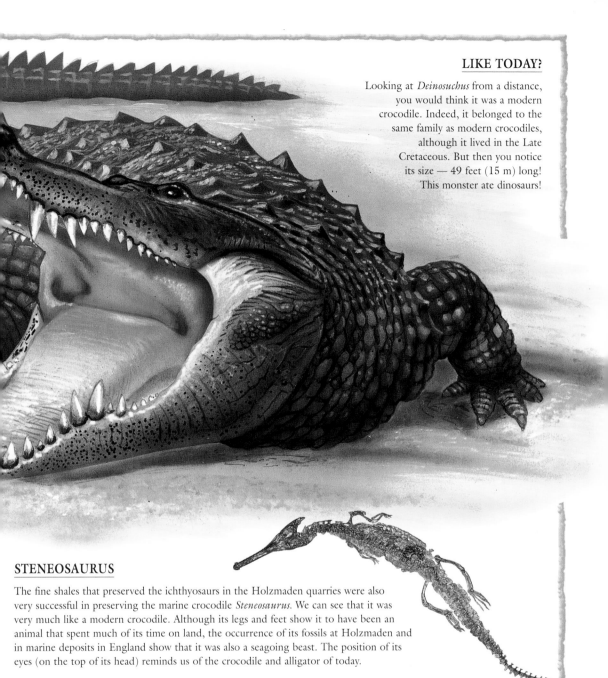

LIKE TODAY?

Looking at *Deinosuchus* from a distance, you would think it was a modern crocodile. Indeed, it belonged to the same family as modern crocodiles, although it lived in the Late Cretaceous. But then you notice its size — 49 feet (15 m) long! This monster ate dinosaurs!

STENEOSAURUS

The fine shales that preserved the ichthyosaurs in the Holzmaden quarries were also very successful in preserving the marine crocodile *Steneosaurus*. We can see that it was very much like a modern crocodile. Although its legs and feet show it to have been an animal that spent much of its time on land, the occurrence of its fossils at Holzmaden and in marine deposits in England show that it was also a seagoing beast. The position of its eyes (on the top of its head) reminds us of the crocodile and alligator of today.

MODERN GHARIAL

In life, *Steneosaurus* must have looked very much like the modern gharial of the Indian rivers — the same long narrow jaws with the many sharp fish-catching teeth, the same long body and tail, and the same short legs. The gharial is a river animal, however, while *Steneosaurus* hunted in the sea.

TRIASSIC	EARLY/MID JURASSIC	LATE JURASSIC	EARLY CRETACEOUS	LATE CRETACEOUS
248-206 MYA	206-159 MYA	159-144 MYA	144-97 MYA	97-65 MYA

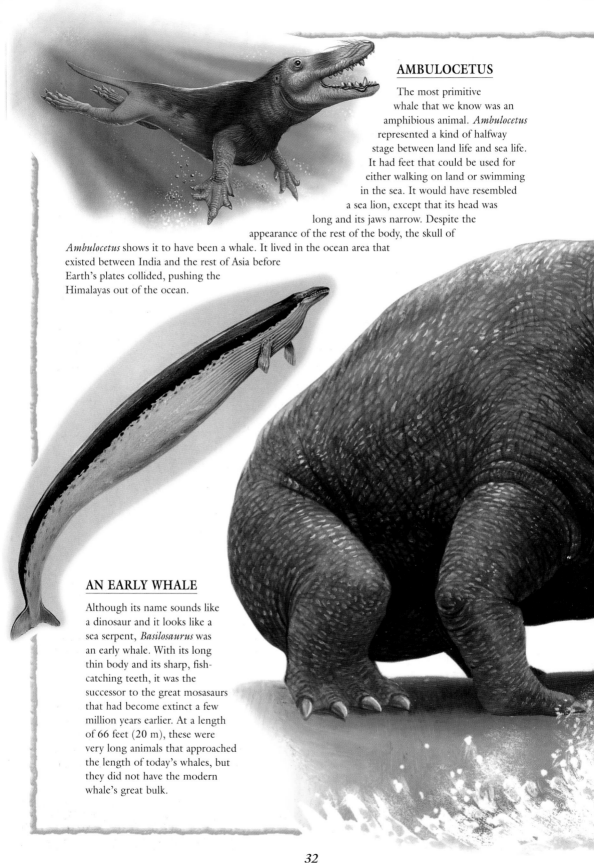

AMBULOCETUS

The most primitive
whale that we know was an
amphibious animal. *Ambulocetus*
represented a kind of halfway
stage between land life and sea life.
It had feet that could be used for
either walking on land or swimming
in the sea. It would have resembled
a sea lion, except that its head was
long and its jaws narrow. Despite the
appearance of the rest of the body, the skull of
Ambulocetus shows it to have been a whale. It lived in the ocean area that
existed between India and the rest of Asia before
Earth's plates collided, pushing the
Himalayas out of the ocean.

AN EARLY WHALE

Although its name sounds like
a dinosaur and it looks like a
sea serpent, *Basilosaurus* was
an early whale. With its long
thin body and its sharp, fish-
catching teeth, it was the
successor to the great mosasaurs
that had become extinct a few
million years earlier. At a length
of 66 feet (20 m), these were
very long animals that approached
the length of today's whales, but
they did not have the modern
whale's great bulk.

WHAT CAME NEXT?

The great extinction event at the end of the Cretaceous Period that wiped out the dinosaurs and other big land-living animals had an even greater effect on the sea. A vast number of the invertebrates (including the ammonites and the belemnites) disappeared, and with them went the big reptiles. The placodonts and the ichthyosaurs had already died out, but suddenly the elasmosaurs, the pliosaurs, and the mosasaurs disappeared, too, as did the pterosaurs that winged their way overhead. This left the oceans wide open to be repopulated by something else — mammals.

INSTEAD OF THE PLESIOSAURS

Sea lions today remind us of plesiosaurs as they pursue fish using the flying movements of their flippers. Even more striking is the resemblance between the ancient ichthyosaurs and dolphins, especially in the similarity of their shapes.

A TEMPORARY MEASURE

As mammals established their supremacy on our planet, a peculiar group of sea mammals cropped up. Called the desmostylians, they were as big as horses. They had strange, stumpy, inward-turned feet that they probably used for walking across the seabed like a hippopotamus. Their teeth consisted of a bunch of forward-pointing tusks forming a structure that resembles a shovel. These were probably used for grazing seaweed or even plucking shellfish, and crushing teeth at the back of the jaws would have been suitable for either. The desmostylians were a short-lived group and died out without leaving any descendants. Other than noticing their resemblance to the walrus, we cannot really compare them with anything that is alive today.

LATE JURASSIC 159-144 MYA	EARLY CRETACEOUS 144-97 MYA	LATE CRETACEOUS 97-65 MYA	PALEOGENE 65-23 MYA	NEOGENE 23-2 MYA

DID YOU KNOW?

• Animals that look similar to each other can be entirely unrelated. Based on a concept known as "convergent evolution," particular shapes fit animals for their particular lifestyles in their particular environments. The same shapes can be seen, however, in different animal species. A classic example of this phenomenon is the shape of ichthyosaurs, sharks, and dolphins. Although these creatures are similar in appearance, one is a reptile, one is a fish, and one is a mammal.

"Parallel evolution" is a similar concept in that some animals from the same ancestors have developed in distinctly different ways. Freshwater, semi-aquatic animals, such as phytosaurs, chasmosaurs, and crocodiles, for example, all have the same shape and the same reptile ancestors, but they have evolved quite differently.

• Water animals adjust their buoyancy in different ways. Deep divers, such as whales, ichthyosaurs, and seals, have heavy bodies and small lungs. In contrast, animals that walk on the seabed, such as placodonts, desmostylans, and dugongs, have heavy bones and large lungs. Animals that "fly" underwater, such as sea lions, plesiosaurs, and penguins, swallow stones to adjust their buoyancy.

• Some sea animals in existence today are bigger than any sea animals of the past. At 93 feet (28 m), the blue whale is much larger than any extinct sea animal known. The biggest giant squid that has been measured is 65 feet (20 m) long, although evidence suggests that even bigger ones exist at depths that have never been seen by science. No animal in the fossil record tops this animal in size.

MORE BOOKS TO READ

3-D Dinosaurs. Eyewitness series.
(Dorling Kindersley)

Children's Guide to Dinosaurs and Other Prehistoric Animals. Philip Whitfield (Simon & Schuster)

Dinosaurs, Spitfires, and Sea Dragons. Christopher McGowan (Harvard)

The Great Marine Reptiles. Development of the Earth series. Andreu Llamas and Luis Rizo (Chelsea House)

Prehistoric Fish. Prehistoric Sea Life. Listen and Color Library. (Spizzirri)

The Ultimate Book of Dinosaurs. Steve Parker (Dempsey Parr)

GLOSSARY

ammonites: extinct, mollusklike marine animals of the Mesozoic age that had flat spiral shells.

aquatic: living or growing in or near water.

ballast: weight that produces stability and control.

bivalve: a mollusk, such as an oyster or a clam, that has a shell made of two parts, or valves, joined with a flexible elastic hinge.

buoyancy: the tendency to float or rise when submerged in a liquid.

continental drift: the theory that Earth's landmasses moved slowly, over billions of years, to form the continents that exist today.

evolution: the theory that organisms change form and develop over long periods of time, so that decendants look or behave differently than their early ancestors.

flanges: ridges or collarlike projections on the edges of some objects that add strength and to which other objects can be attached.

gastroliths: stones found in the stomach of an animal that were taken in to assist digestion or to provide sea animals with additional weight to keep them underwater.

gharial: a large reptile from India that looks like an alligator but has a long, narrow snout instead of a broad one.

invertebrate: a living organism that does not have a backbone.

metabolic: related to the processes within living organisms by which chemical changes convert food into energy.

mollusks: invertebrate animals, such as oysters, clams, and snails, that have a soft body protected by a hard shell.

"Nessie":: the nickname given to a dinosaurlike beast that is rumored to exist in Loch Ness, a freshwater lake in northern Scotland.

newt: a small, semiaquatic salamander.

Pangaea: the single mass of land that existed on Earth in prehistoric times, before the continents drifted apart.

plate tectonics: the theory that Earth's continents once were a single landmass that drifted or was forced apart over billions of years.

platypus: a small, semiaquatic mammal, found only in Australia, that has webbed feet, a ducklike bill, and a broad, flat, beaverlike tail. Although it has hair on its body and feeds its young with milk, like other mammals, it reproduces by laying eggs, like birds or reptiles.

quarries: large open pits or excavations of land that are dug out to obtain stone, sand, or gravel.

reptile: a cold-blooded, egg-laying vertebrate, such as a snake, a turtle, or a crocodile, that has scales or horny plates on its body.

scavenged: cleared away or removed from an area, or taken as matter to feed on.

sediment: material that is suspended in a liquid and, when undisturbed, settles to the bottom.

skull: the bony framework of the head, also called the cranium.

struts: bars or rods used to brace a structure against pressure along its length.

taphonomy: the study of the processes by which organisms become fossils.

vertebrate: a living organism that has a backbone, or spinal column.

INDEX

ACKNOWLEDGEMENTS

The original publisher would like to thank Advocate, Helen Wire, www.fossilfinds.com, and Elizabeth Wiggans for their assistance.

Picture Credits: t=top, b=bottom, c=center, l=left, r=right
Lisa Alderson: 5b, 8-9c, 17t, 18-19c, 24-25c, 30c. John Alston: 4b, 8tl, 9r, 10b, 11br, 13t, 18t, 20l, 21t, 25t, 26l, 26b, 28t. BBC Natural History Unit: 5tr, 11t, 12tl, 15cr, 28cr, 31b. Corbis: 13b, 28b. Steve Etches: 14tl. Fossil Finds: 8b, 22t, 28cl. Simon Mendez: front cover, 4c, 10-11c, 12-13c, 16-17c, 21cr, 21br, 26-27, 26-29c, 30b, 32-33c. Natural History Museum: 16t, 19t, 24b, 27t, 31bc, 32cl. Bob Nicholls: 14-15c. Peterborough Museum: 15b. Luis Rey: 10t, 20-21c, 30-31c, 32t. Royal Tyrell Museum: 25cr. Science Photo Library: 18b. University of Bristol: 23b. University of Toronto: 4t.

Every effort has been made to trace the copyright holders, and we apologize in advance for any unintentional errors or omissions.

DINOSAURS

IN THE SKY

by Dougal Dixon

Gareth Stevens Publishing
A WORLD ALMANAC EDUCATION GROUP COMPANY

CONTENTS

Please visit our web site at:
www.garethstevens.com
For a free color catalog describing Gareth
Stevens' list of high-quality books and
multimedia programs, call 1-800-542-2595
(USA) or 1-800-387-3178 (Canada). Gareth
Stevens Publishing's Fax: (414) 332-3567.

Library of Congress Cataloging-in-Publication Data
available upon request from publisher. Fax (414) 336-0157
or the attention of the Publishing Records Department.

ISBN 0-8368-3329-5

First North American book fair edition published
in 2002, first Norh American editions published in
2001 as two volumes, In the Sea and In the Sky, by
Gareth Stevens Publishing
A World Almanac Education Group Company
330 West Olive Street, Suite 100
Milwaukee, WI 53212 USA

U.S. editions © 2001 by Gareth Stevens, Inc. First
published by ticktock Publishing Ltd., Century
Place, Lamberts Road, Tunbridge Wells, Kent TN2
3EH, U.K. Original editions © 2001 by ticktock
Publishing Ltd. Additional end matter © 2001 by
Gareth Stevens, Inc.

Illustrations: John Alston, Lisa Alderson,
Simon Mendez, Luis Rey
Gareth Stevens editor: David K. Wright
Cover design: Katherine A. Goedheer
Consultant: Paul Mayer, Geology Collections
Manager, Milwaukee Public Museum

All rights reserved. No part of this book may
be reproduced, stored in a retrieval system, or
transmitted in any form or by any means,
electronic, mechanical, photocopying, recording,
or otherwise, without the prior written permission
of the copyright holder.

Printed in Hong Kong

2 3 4 5 6 7 8 9 06 05 04 03 02

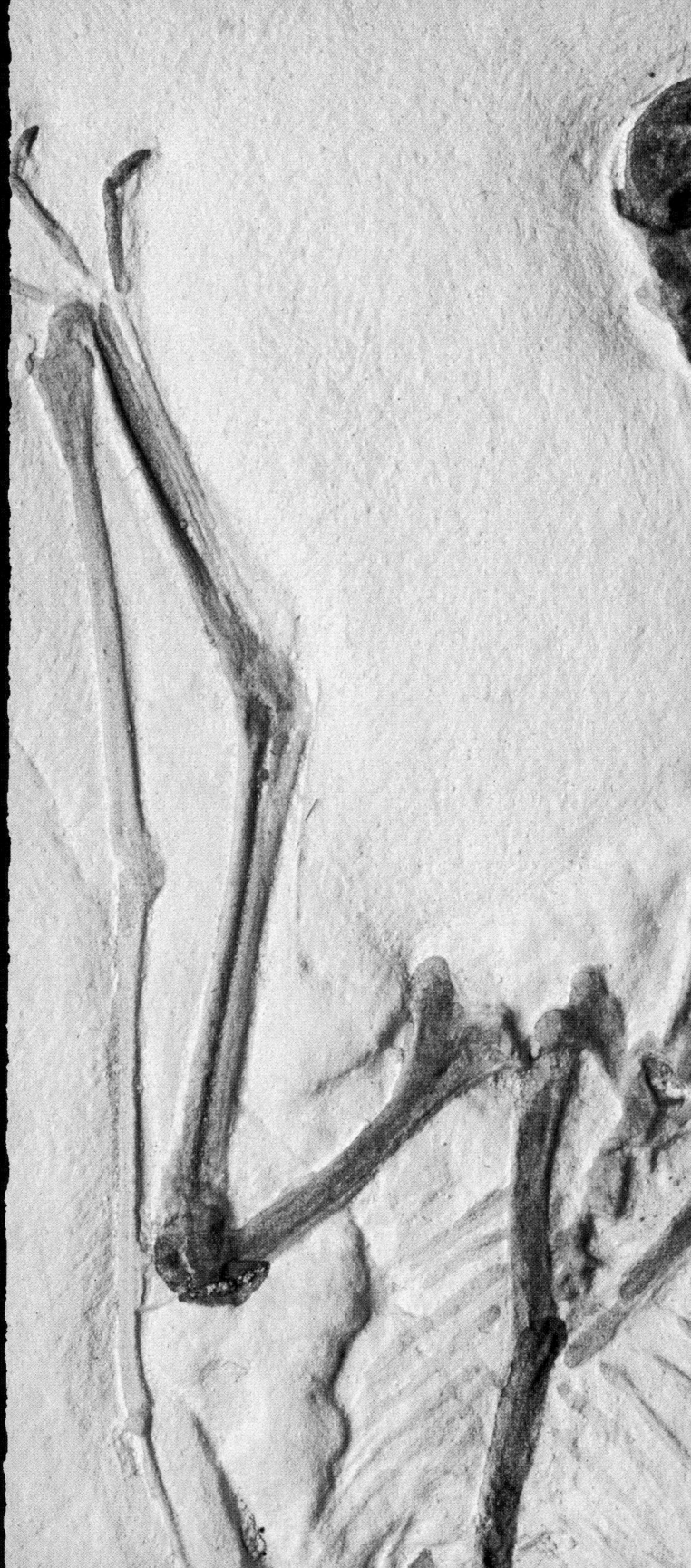

IN THE SKY

WING AND A PRAYER

The earliest flying reptile known was the Late Permian *Coelurosauravus*. It looked very much like a lizard, but its ribs were extended to the side and supported gliding wings made of skin. The modern flying lizard of Malaysia glides in exactly the same manner as *Coelurosauravus*.

KING OF THE SKIES

By Late Triassic times, gliders like *Coelurosauravus* had been replaced in importance by the pterosaurs. These famous flying reptiles were the first vertebrates to adapt to a life of active flight. They appeared at about the same time as the first dinosaurs and became extinct at the end of the Cretaceous Period. Pterosaur wings were made of reinforced skin stretched out on an arm and an elongated fourth finger.

EARLY BIRDS

Birds such as this *Sinornis* appeared about halfway through the time of the dinosaurs, evolving from the dinosaurs themselves. Birds continue to thrive and are the main flying vertebrates today. Their wings are made of a bony structure consisting of some of the fingers fused together and supporting feathers that fan from the arms.

THE PIONEERS

While the dinosaurs, fish, and mammals were colonizing the land and the sea in prehistoric times, the sky above was buzzing with activity. Early flyers were simple organisms, but nature gradually came up with more complex designs. First came the insects, which continue to flourish today. Next came the flying reptiles, gliding creatures that evolved from ground-living, lizardlike animals. These reptiles were replaced in importance by the pterosaurs, probably the most famous of the ancient flying reptiles. Finally, the first birds appeared halfway through the time of the dinosaurs and have continued to rule the skies to this day.

AMBER PERFECTION

The best fossils come from amber preservation. When an unwary insect gets stuck in the sticky resin that oozes from tree trunks, the resin engulfs the insect and preserves it perfectly. When the tree dies and becomes buried over a long period of time, the resin solidifies and becomes the mineral we call amber. The 1994 film *Jurassic Park* was based on the premise that foreign DNA could be taken from biting insects preserved in amber to recreate the creature that was bitten. While this might not be possible today, it is an exciting concept.

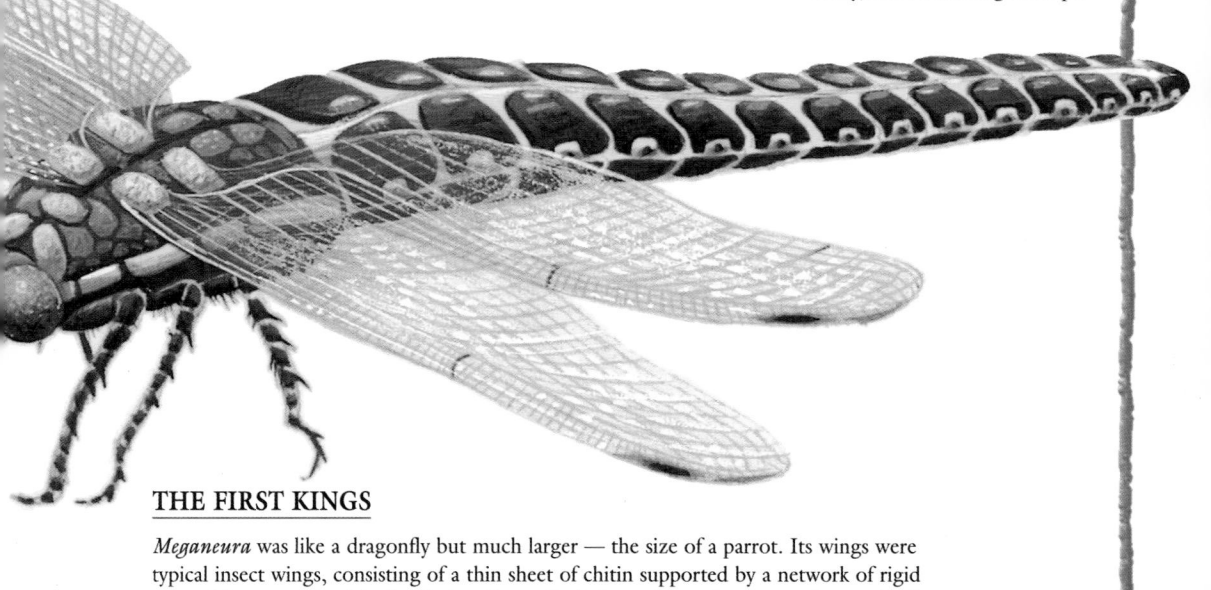

THE FIRST KINGS

Meganeura was like a dragonfly but much larger — the size of a parrot. Its wings were typical insect wings, consisting of a thin sheet of chitin supported by a network of rigid veins. *Meganeura* lived in the Carboniferous Period, not long after insects first evolved.

CARBONIFEROUS/PERMIAN	TRIASSIC	EARLY/MID JURASSIC	LATE JURASSIC	EARLY/LATE CRETACEOUS
354-290/290-248 MYA	248-206 MYA	206-159 MYA	159-144 MYA	144-65 MYA

SOLAR POWERED

Kuehneosaurus, a gliding
reptile that existed in western
England in the Late Triassic, was very similar
in structure to *Icarosaurus*. There were about a
dozen wing supports (about half the number of
the earlier *Coelurosauravus*), suggesting that the
wings were longer and narrower and probably more
maneuverable. The skin of the wings was probably
rich in blood vessels, and the wings may have helped
warm up the animal in the sun like a solar panel.

LONG LEGS

Late Triassic *Sharovipteryx* from central
Asia was a small lizardlike animal about
the size of a sparrow. It had the most
ridiculous-looking hind legs, each one
longer than the complete length of the
body. These long legs only made sense
when scientists noticed the imprint of
a membrane of skin stretched between
the legs and the middle of the tail.

SHAROVIPTERYX IN FLIGHT

When alive, *Sharovipteryx* must have been able to glide using
the wings on its hind legs. This would not have been a very
stable type of flight, but it was probably efficient to transport
the reptile from one tree to another. Small skin flaps on the
forelimbs would have helped control the flight. With the wing
membrane stretched on elongated limbs, *Sharovipteryx* must
have resembled a back-to-front pterosaur. Some scientists have even
suggested that it may have been among the pterosaurs' early relatives.

EARLY FLYING REPTILES

The simplest kind of flight is a gliding flight — one that needs little muscular effort. All that is required is a lightness of body and some kind of structure that catches the air and allows the body to be carried along upon it, like a paper airplane. In modern times, we see this structure in flying squirrels, flying lizards, and even flying frogs. A number of flying reptiles populated the skies in Permian and Triassic times, and each one evolved independently from different reptile ancestors.

LONGISQUAMA

This fossil of the flying reptile *Longisquama* comes from Late Triassic central Asia. It had a completely different type of flying mechanism. A double row of long scales stuck up along the backbone, each scale forming a shallow V-shape along its midline. When spread, the scales would have overlapped like the feathers of birds (which appeared 60 million years later) to give a continuous gliding surface.

SCALES

A FAMOUS FIND

Three schoolboys in New Jersey discovered a famous specimen of Late Triassic *Icarosaurus*. The partial skeleton shows it to have been a lizardlike animal with long projections from its ribs. The angles at which the rib extensions lay suggested that the wings could have been folded back out of the way when the animal was at rest. Several decades after the discovery, one of the finders realized that under U.S. law the specimen belonged to those who made the discovery, and the specimen is now lost to science, having disappeared into a private collection.

PERMIAN 290-248 MYA	TRIASSIC 248-206 MYA	EARLY/MID JURASSIC 206-159 MYA	LATE JURASSIC 159-144 MYA	EARLY/LATE CRETACEOUS 144-65 MYA

SWIMMING PTEROSAURS

In 1784, some scientists put forward the idea that pterosaurs were not flying animals but swimming animals. This theory influenced many scientists and artists, including Johann Wagler, whose 1830 sketch (left) suggested that pterosaurs were an intermediate stage between mammals and birds.

DEVILISH PTEROSAURS

In 1840, British geologist Thomas Hawkins published a book on the fossil sea reptiles (the ichthyosaurs and plesiosaurs) that had been discovered up to that time. The frontispiece of the book was an engraving by John Martin, an English painter of biblical and historical subjects. It was a nightmare scene in which he depicted monstrous ichthyosaurs, plesiosaurs, and pterosaurs that resembled bat-winged demons.

FURRY PTEROSAURS

A surprisingly modern interpretation of pterosaurs was drawn in 1843 by Edward Newman. He regarded pterosaurs as flying marsupials. Although the mouse ears are inaccurate, the furry bodies and the predatory lifestyle are in keeping with how we now regard these creatures.

VICTORIAN TERRORS

The concrete pterosaurs (or "pterodactyles" as they were then called) erected on the grounds of the Crystal Palace in south London in 1854 tell us that most Victorians still viewed these creatures as winged dragons. These statues were more delicate than the surrounding statues of dinosaurs and sea animals, and unfortunately most were badly damaged or destroyed by the 1930s.

THE DISCOVERY OF THE PTEROSAURS

The first pterosaur fossil to have been scientifically studied was an almost perfect skeleton from the lithographic limestone quarries of Solnhofen, Germany, discovered between 1767 and 1784 (*see pages 10–11*). Although the skeleton was nearly complete, it was impossible to compare it with any animal alive at the time, so the find remained a mystery. Seventeen years later, the French pioneer naturalist Baron Georges Cuvier guessed that it was a flying reptile. Since that date, scientists have come up with many different ideas of what pterosaurs were and how they lived.

JURASSIC BATS?

English geologist Sir Henry De la Beche produced a drawing in 1830 showing animal life in the Jurassic (then called Liassic) sea of southern England. Life in the sea consisted of swimming reptiles, fish, and ammonites. In the air were flying pterosaurs, which De la Beche depicted as batlike creatures, with their wing membranes stretching all the way to their feet.

THE MODERN QUARRIES

Centuries ago, Romans excavated the fine limestone from the Solnhofen quarries to make tiles and paving stones. In the 18th century, the fine-grained surface of the rock was found to be ideal for printing. This discovery led to the rapid expansion of the quarries. Despite the fact that these quarries are famous for their fossils (not only of pterosaurs, but of early birds, small dinosaurs, lizards, and a whole host of marine animals), it takes the removal of a vast volume of rock to find one worthwhile skeleton.

NORTHERN EUROPE

SHALLOW WATERS (MODERN SOUTHERN GERMANY)

REEF

TETHYS OCEAN

SOLNHOFEN

Over millions of years, the surface of Earth has changed due to the action of plate tectonics, the name given to the activity that occurs beneath Earth's surface. Hot magma rises, forcing our planet to tear on the surface and separating previously joined landmasses. In Late Jurassic times, the area of southern Germany, including Solnhofen, lay in the shallows along the northern edge of the Tethys Ocean. This ocean separated Europe from Africa. Today all that is left of the Tethys is the Mediterranean Sea and the drying puddles of the Black Sea, the Caspian Sea, and the Aral Sea, all flanked by the mountains that were pushed out of the ground as the continents collided.

ANATOMY OF A LAGOON

Along the edge of the continental shelf to the north of the Tethys Ocean, a vast reef of sponges grew in deeper waters. Remains of this reef can now be found stretching from Spain to Romania. As it approached the surface, this reef stopped growing as the sponges died and coral reefs started to grow on top of them. Eventually, a series of lagoons was formed between the reef and the land. Low islands lay across the lagoon, and these were arid, with only a few scraggly plants. The stagnant water in the lagoon became poisonous and killed any animal that swam or fell into it. Because fine sediment was accumulating below, these animals were preserved almost perfectly at the bottom of the lagoon.

TRIASSIC 248-206 MYA	EARLY/MID JURASSIC 206-159 MYA	LATE JURASSIC 159-144 MYA	EARLY CRETACEOUS 144-97 MYA	LATE CRETACEOUS 97-65 MYA

SOLNHOFEN - PTEROSAUR PARADISE

Solnhofen in southern Germany has produced a treasure trove of finds — fossils in such wonderful condition that every detail of even the most delicate of organisms can still be seen. The rock is made of very fine particles and was formed under conditions totally lacking in oxygen, so no further decay took place. The technical name that geologists give to such fossil occurrences is *lagerstatten.* Only about a dozen such sites are known, and most people regard Solnhofen as the best in the world.

THE HEADLESS ONES

Many of the pterosaur fossils found at Solnhofen are without their heads.

The probable reason is that when the pterosaurs died they fell into the shallow waters along the northern edge of the Tethys Ocean.

When the pterosaurs landed on the lagoon, they floated at the surface for a while because their bodies were so lightweight.

While lying on the surface, their floating bodies began to decay and their heads, being the heaviest part, fell off first.

Eventually, after their heads had fallen off, the rest of the pterosaurs' bodies sank to the lagoon floor, where they were quickly covered by fine sediment.

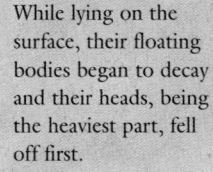

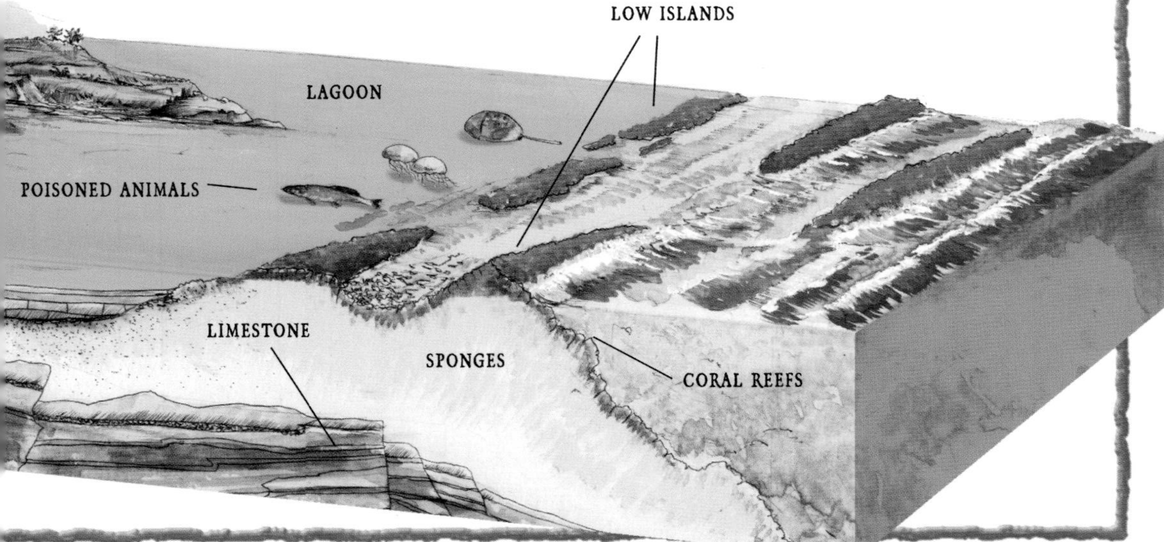

LOW ISLANDS

LAGOON

POISONED ANIMALS

LIMESTONE

SPONGES

CORAL REEFS

NARROW WINGS
PRODUCING ACTIVE,
FLAPPING FLIGHT

THE FANTASY

Many works of fiction, including
the film *One Million Years BC*, show
pterosaurs carrying away heavy prey like
human beings in their feet or their jaws.
Even if human beings had been around at that
time, the pterosaurs would have been unable to do
this without severely disrupting their center of balance.

AN EDUCATED GUESS

Two good fossils of
Eudimorphodon are known.
They both have the wings
folded to the body, but the
wing membrane has not been
preserved. Nor is there any
direct evidence of a furry pelt.
We can, however, guess what
the membrane and the fur
were like by comparing the
fossils with pterosaurs that
were better preserved
(*see pages 14–15*).

LONG TAIL

TRIASSIC 248-206 MYA	EARLY/MID JURASSIC 206-159 MYA	LATE JURASSIC 159-144 MYA	EARLY CRETACEOUS 144-97 MYA	LATE CRETACEOUS 97-65 MYA

EUDIMORPHODON

Eudimorphodon had all the physical attributes of the rhamphorhynchoids. It had long, narrow wings made of skin supported by rods of gristle and a wing span of about 3 feet (1 meter). Because of its variety of teeth, it could easily catch and eat fish, and its furry body kept this creature warm and helped make possible its constantly active lifestyle.

SHORT
WRIST
BONES

TEETH OF
DIFFERENT
SIZES

FURRY
BODY

THE EARLIEST PTEROSAUR

The pterosaurs were the most important of the flying animals in Triassic, Jurassic, and Cretaceous times. Once they evolved, they quickly adopted all the features that were to remain with the group for the rest of their existence. Pterosaurs fall into two groups. The more primitive group — the rhamphorhynchoids — had long tails, short wrist bones, and narrow wings. Appearing in Triassic times, they were the first to evolve.

The other group — the pterodactyloids — evolved later, toward the end of the Jurassic.

WING MUSCLES

Pterosaurs must have had a flying action like that of modern bats or birds (right). The arrangement of their shoulder bones and wing bones show that the muscles facilitated active, flapping flight.

CATCHING PREY

Many pterosaurs caught fish, and, judging by its teeth, *Eudimorphodon* was one of them. The balance of the animal in flight was so delicate that it would not have been able to fly with a fish in its mouth. The pterosaur had to have swallowed the fish immediately to get it to its center of balance.

DIMORPHODON SKELETON

The skeletons of *Dimorphodon* fall to pieces and are crushed easily, because they are made up of the finest struts of bone. Nevertheless, two good *Dimorphodon* specimens have been found, both of them now in the Natural History Museum in London.

JURASSIC SKIES

Above the Early Jurassic shorelines the air was thick with wheeling pterosaurs. They were all of the long-tailed rhamphorhynchoid type. Within a few million years these creatures would be replaced by a new pterosaur group — the short-tailed, long-necked, long-wristed pterodactyloids.

BIG HEADS

Rhamphorhynchoid pterosaurs ruled the skies during the early Jurassic Period. The earliest Jurassic pterosaur known was discovered in 1828 by the famous professional collector Mary Anning. It was given the name *Dimorphodon* because of its two types of teeth. Scientists today are still in disagreement over many of its features. These disagreements are typical of our lack of knowledge of the pterosaurs in general.

BRILLIANT BEAK

Dimorphodon had two different types of teeth that were good for grabbing and holding slippery prey such as fish. The skull was very high and narrow and consisted of windows separated by fine struts of bone. The sides of the head were very likely brightly colored for signaling, just like the beaks of modern tall-beaked birds, such as puffins or toucans.

ON THE GROUND

We know that pterosaurs like *Dimorphodon* were very adept at flight, but we are not sure how they moved around when they were not flying. The old theory was that pterosaurs crawled like lizards, while some scientists saw them as running on their hind legs like birds, with their wings folded out of the way. However, footprints in lake sediments from South America attributed to pterosaurs show the marks of the hind feet walking in a narrow track, with marks seemingly made by the claws of the forelimbs in a wider track on each side. This suggests that pterosaurs were walking upright, using the arms like crutches or walking sticks. A final theory suggests that because of their similarity to bats, perhaps they did not come to the ground at all but hung upside down from trees.

TRIASSIC	EARLY/MID JURASSIC	LATE JURASSIC	EARLY CRETACEOUS	LATE CRETACEOUS
248-206 MYA	206-159 MYA	159-144 MYA	144-97 MYA	97-65 MYA

SOFT COVERINGS

Most fossils are of sea-living animals, because sea-living animals have a better chance of falling to the seabed and eventually becoming entombed in sedimentary rock. However, many pterosaurs lived in coastal areas or around lakes and fell into the water when they died. Sometimes they were fossilized in environments that preserved the finest of details, such as wing membranes and fur.

WING STRUCTURE

The wing membrane of a pterosaur was stiffened by fine rods of gristle that fanned out from the arm and hand to the wing's trailing edge. The pattern of the gristle stiffening is the same as the arrangement of a bird's flight feathers and the supporting fingers of a bat's wing.

A MODERN INTERPRETATION?

Many think that birds are the modern equivalent of the pterosaurs. The pterosaur has more in common with the modern bat than with any bird, however, particularly with its fur and membranous wings. Pterosaurs and birds shared the Cretaceous skies, but bats did not evolve until pterosaurs died out.

THE BEST PRESERVED

This *Rhamphorhynchus* from the Solnhofen deposits in Germany is one of the best preserved pterosaur fossils we have. Even the structure of its wing membrane is visible.

TRIASSIC	EARLY/MID JURASSIC	LATE JURASSIC	EARLY CRETACEOUS	LATE CRETACEOUS
248-206 MYA	206-159 MYA	159-144 MYA	144-97 MYA	97-65 MYA

HOW WERE THE WINGS ATTACHED?

A great deal of uncertainty surrounds the question of just how the pterosaur's wings were attached to the animal. Some scientists think that the wings stretched from the arms and fourth finger to the body and did not touch the hind limbs. Other scientists think that the wings were attached to the hind limbs at the knee. Others feel that the wings may have stretched right down to the ankles.

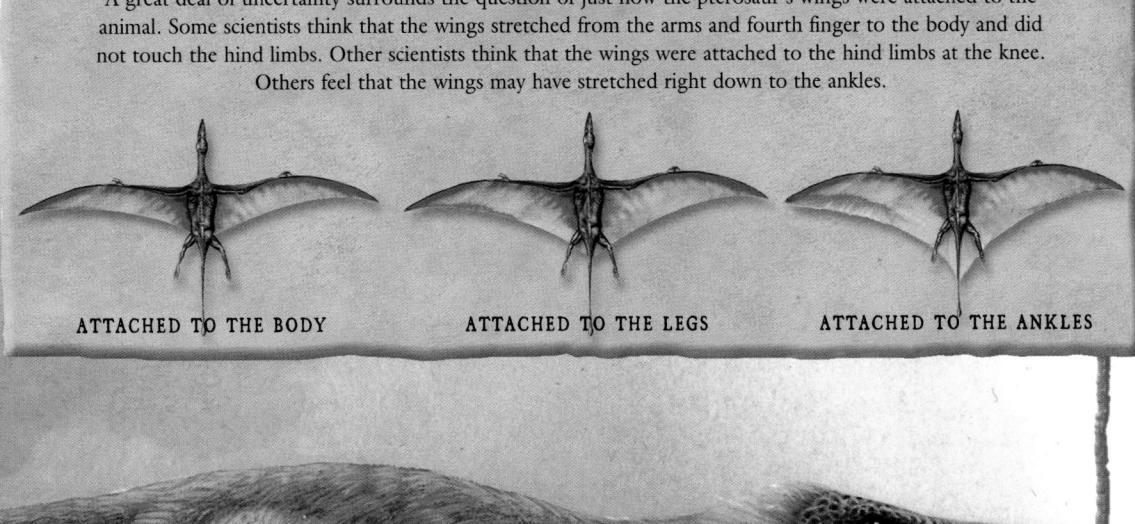

ATTACHED TO THE BODY   ATTACHED TO THE LEGS   ATTACHED TO THE ANKLES

FURRY PTEROSAUR

The fossilized remains of the rhamphorhynchoid *Sordes*, discovered among late Jurassic lake deposits in Kazakhstan in 1971, proved what many paleontologists had thought for a long time — that the pterosaurs were covered with hair. The sediment was so fine and the fossilization was so complete that not only was the wing membrane preserved, but fibrous patches were visible on the whole of the body, except for the tail. The diamond-shaped flap of skin at the end of the long, stiff tail was probably used for steering or for balancing as the animal flew.

When the British scientist Charles Darwin visited the Galapagos islands in the 19th century, he was struck by the variety of different beak shapes among one species of finch. Different shapes supported different lifestyles — heavy beaks for cracking seeds and short beaks for pecking insects, and so on. This revelation trigged Darwin's theory of evolution — the idea that, over millions of years, creatures could evolve to adapt to their surroundings. The variation in shape of the various *Pterodactylus* species fits in perfectly with Darwin's theory.

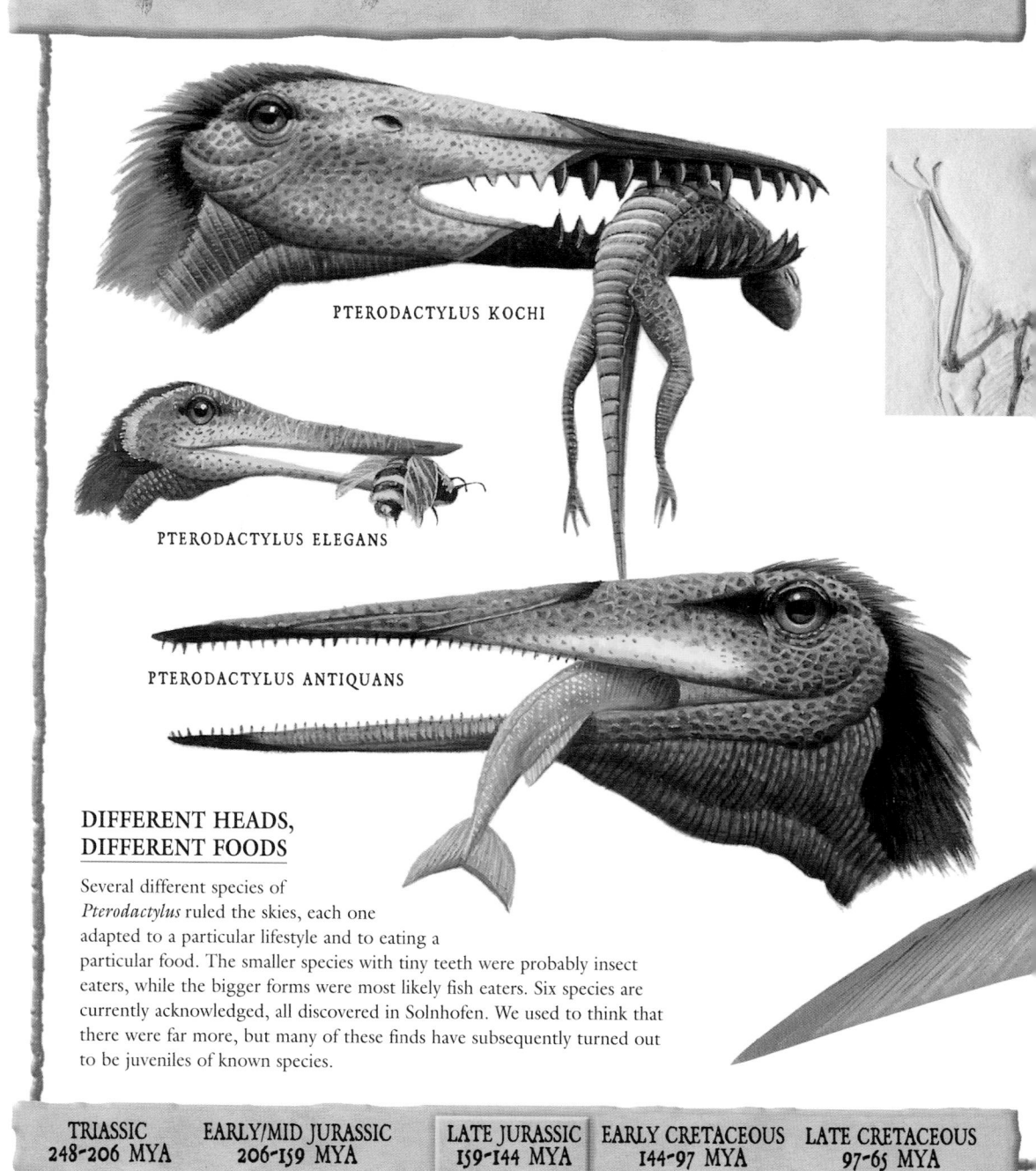

PTERODACTYLUS KOCHI

PTERODACTYLUS ELEGANS

PTERODACTYLUS ANTIQUANS

DIFFERENT HEADS, DIFFERENT FOODS

Several different species of *Pterodactylus* ruled the skies, each one adapted to a particular lifestyle and to eating a particular food. The smaller species with tiny teeth were probably insect eaters, while the bigger forms were most likely fish eaters. Six species are currently acknowledged, all discovered in Solnhofen. We used to think that there were far more, but many of these finds have subsequently turned out to be juveniles of known species.

TRIASSIC 248-206 MYA	EARLY/MID JURASSIC 206-159 MYA	LATE JURASSIC 159-144 MYA	EARLY CRETACEOUS 144-97 MYA	LATE CRETACEOUS 97-65 MYA

THE MOST FAMOUS

It is *Pterodactylus* that gives the pterodactyloid group its name. In fact, pterosaurs are commonly referred to as "pterodactyls." The pterodactyloids dominated in Late Jurassic times, but there have been several different types found dating from this time, so their evolution must have been under way somewhat earlier.

PTERODACTYLUS FOSSIL

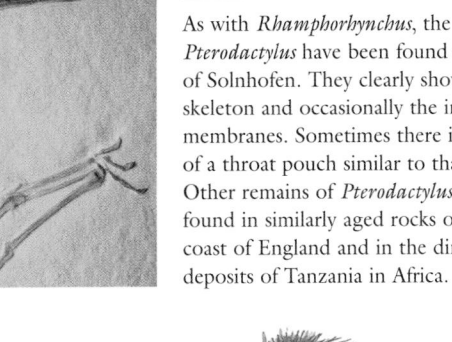

As with *Rhamphorhynchus*, the best specimens of *Pterodactylus* have been found in the limestone deposits of Solnhofen. They clearly show the details of the skeleton and occasionally the imprints of the wing membranes. Sometimes there is even the imprint of a throat pouch similar to that of a pelican. Other remains of *Pterodactylus* have been found in similarly aged rocks on the south coast of England and in the dinosaur-rich deposits of Tanzania in Africa.

PTERODACTYLUS IN FLIGHT

Most agree that pterodactyloids originally evolved from rhamphorhynchoids, but *Pterodactylus* does display several differences from the group. Its head and neck are longer than in the rhamphorhynchoids. The head meets the neck at a right angle, rather than in a straight line, and its skull is more lightly built. It has a short tail, with no steering or flying function, and its long wrist bones mean that the three fingers of the "hand" are farther down the wing.

A QUESTION OF CRESTS

Many pterosaurs had spectacular crests that allowed
them to signal to one another and identify members
of their own species.

Pteranodon, with its
backward-pointing crest, is
the most famous of the crested
pterosaurs. Its crest may have
helped it steer as it flew.

PTERANODON

Tropeognathus had
semicircular crests on its
upper and lower jaws. This
crest arrangement may have
helped divide the water as
the pterosaur dipped into
the waves for fish.

TROPEOGNATHUS

TAPEJARA

Tapejara was characterized
by a tall, bony crest at
the front of its skull,
probably supporting
a flap of skin behind.

TUPUXUARA

Tupuxuara had a crest that consisted of a vast
plate of bone reaching up and beyond the
back of the skull. It was full of blood
vessels and so must have been
covered by skin. Perhaps it
had a heat-regulating
function as well as
being used for
display.

HEADS & CRESTS

Birds are in great abundance today. They range from perching birds and swimming birds to wading birds and hunting birds.

Modern birds have a variety of different heads and beaks — deep, strong beaks for cracking nuts; long, pointed beaks for probing mud; short, sharp beaks for pecking insects; and hooked beaks for tearing flesh. This variety was just as pronounced among the pterodactyloids. During their time on Earth, they diversified into different types, with different head shapes to suit different lifestyles.

HIDEOUS FIND

One of the most grotesque of the pterosaurs was *Dsungaripterus*. It had a beak like a pair of upturned forceps, a battery of crushing, toothlike, bony knobs at the back of the jaws and a crest that stretched from the back of the head to the snout. It was a large pterosaur with a wingspan of more than 10 feet (3 m). *Dsungaripterus* was the first pterosaur discovered in China.

DSUNGARIPTERUS RESTORED

We can usually tell how an animal lived and what it ate by looking at its jaws. *Dsungaripterus*, which we think lived in Late Jurassic and Early Cretaceous Africa, probably ate shellfish. The narrow, pointed jaws could have been used for digging out shellfish from rocky crannies, and the shells would have been crushed by the toothlike knobs in the back of their jaws. The crest could have been brightly colored and was probably used for signaling other pterosaurs.

TRIASSIC	EARLY/MID JURASSIC	LATE JURASSIC	EARLY CRETACEOUS	LATE CRETACEOUS
248-206 MYA	206-159 MYA	159-144 MYA	144-97 MYA	97-65 MYA

PTERANODON SKELETON

This partial skeleton of the giant pterosaur *Pteranodon* was found in Cretaceous rocks in Kansas. It shows a skull fragment, the bones of the wing finger, and the complete hind legs. The whole skeleton was extremely light in weight, and the bones had openings to allow oxygen into air sacks connected to the lungs. We see this system in modern birds.

QUETZALCOATLUS

PTERANODON

ARGENTAVIS

A FLIGHT OF MONSTERS

Pteranodon has long been thought of as the largest of the pterosaurs. The biggest species of *Pteranodon* had a wingspan of about 30 feet (9 m). In the 1970s, however, remains from an even larger pterosaur were found in Upper Cretaceous rocks in Texas. It was given the name *Quetzalcoatlus*, after the flying serpent from Aztec mythology. All sorts of estimates were made about the size of this beast. The current estimate is that it had a wingspan of about 36–39 feet (11–12 m). The biggest bird known is the condorlike *Argentavis* from Argentina, which existed around 35 million years ago. It had a wingspan of 25 feet (7.5 m). Among living birds, the royal albatross has the biggest wingspan, reaching 10 feet (3 m).

THE BIGGEST

Pteranodon was discovered in the 1870s in the Upper Cretaceous beds of Kansas. It had a wingspan of more than 30 feet (9 m). This discovery occurred before the age of powered aviation, and science was astounded by the idea that anything this large could fly. Today its size seems fairly modest when we compare it with more recent discoveries.

THE BIGGEST — FOR THE MOMENT

The current record holder is *Arambourgiania*, a pterodactyloid that may have had a wingspan of about 39 feet (12 m). It had an extremely long neck, and when the neck bones were first found they were thought to have been the long finger bones that supported the wing. The original name given to this creature was *Titanopteryx*, but scientists had already given that name to something else, so its title had to be changed.

THE SMALLEST — FOR THE MOMENT

At the other end of the scale, tiny *Anurognathus* holds the record for the smallest known pterosaur. It had a wingspan of about 2 feet (50 centimeters). Its short head contained little peg-like teeth that were ideal for catching and crushing insects. Despite its short pterodactyloid-like tail, it is actually a member of the more primitive rhamphorhynchoids. Only one skeleton has been found, in the Late Jurassic Solnhofen deposits (*see pages 10–11*).

TRIASSIC 248-206 MYA	EARLY/MID JURASSIC 206-159 MYA	LATE JURASSIC 159-144 MYA	EARLY CRETACEOUS 144-97 MYA	LATE CRETACEOUS 97-65 MYA

THE FIRST BIRD

In 1859, Charles Darwin published *The Origin of Species* and created a sensation. How could animals have evolved into different types over a long period if they had all been created at one time, as it says in the Bible? The scientific community found itself in opposition to the overpowering influence of traditional biblical teaching. Then, two years later, a remarkable fossil was discovered in the quarries of Solnhofen (*see pages 10–11*). It was obviously a dinosaur, but it featured bird's wings and was covered with feathers. Here were the remains of a creature that appeared to represent a stage in the evolution of birds from dinosaurs. Today, few scientists dispute the notion that *Archaeopteryx* (as this creature was named) evolved from dinosaur ancestors.

FEATHER

The first *Archaeopteryx* fossil to be found was no more than a feather. By itself, it looks like nothing unusual. It is a perfectly conventional flight feather as found on a modern bird. The main support is a vane that is off-center, showing that it is from a wing and used for flight. The filaments forming the vane of the feather had rows of hooks that enabled them to connect with one another and give stability — just as in a modern bird. A downy portion at the base provided insulation — also as in birds. About a year later, the first partial *Archaeopteryx* skeleton was found.

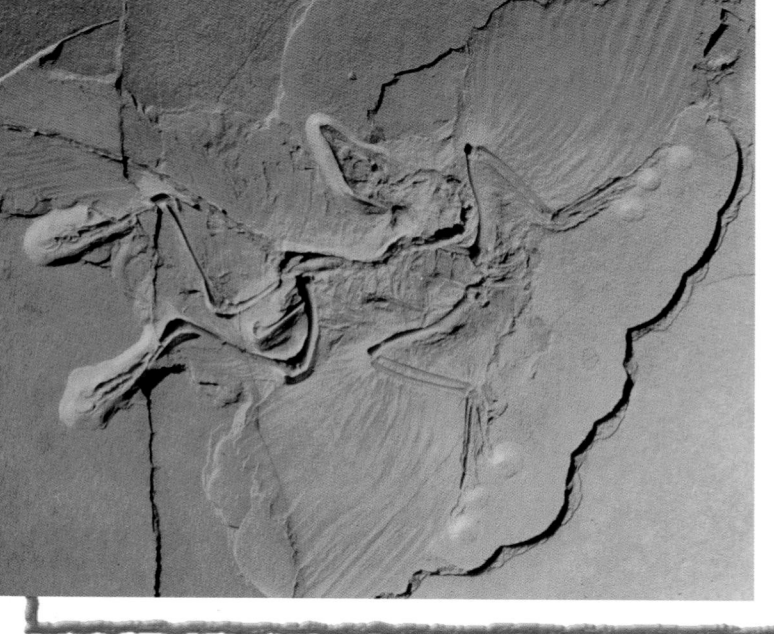

VINDICATING DARWIN

Eight *Archaeopteryx* fossils have been found so far, all from the Solnhofen quarries, ranging in quality from a single feather to an almost complete bony skeleton with feathers. One was found in a private collection, having been misidentified as the small dinosaur *Compsognathus*. This specimen did not show the feathers, and the misidentification points out the resemblance between primitive birds and their dinosaur ancestors.

THE LIVING ARCHAEOPTERYX

Had we seen *Archaeopteryx* in life, fluttering away from us, there would be no doubt in our minds that we were looking at a bird, though a rather clumsy one. However, a closer look would reveal a set of toothed jaws, as in a dinosaur, instead of the usual bird beak. The tail appeared to be paddle-shaped, unlike a modern bird's muscular stump with a bunch of feathers. This tail was a stiff, straight rod, like a dinosaur's tail, with feathers growing from each side. The final oddity would be the claws, three of them protruding from the leading edge of the wing. All in all, *Archaeopteryx* would have appeared part bird, part dinosaur.

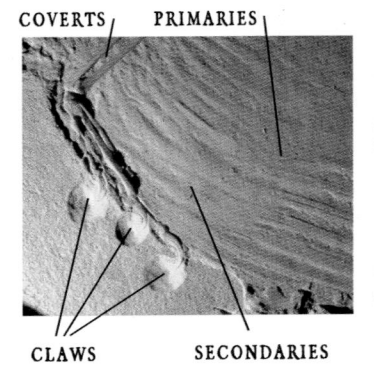

COVERTS PRIMARIES

CLAWS SECONDARIES

THE WING

The wing of *Archaeopteryx* was no halfway measure. Apart from the clawed fingers, it was identical in structure to the wing of a modern flying bird, with the elongated fingerlike primary feathers, bunched secondaries, and coverts streamlining the whole structure. The wing muscles would have been weaker than those of a modern bird, since there was no strong breastbone to anchor them. But the flying action must have been the same.

TRIASSIC 248-206 MYA	EARLY/MID JURASSIC 206-159 MYA	LATE JURASSIC 159-144 MYA	EARLY CRETACEOUS 144-97 MYA	LATE CRETACEOUS 97-65 MYA

CAUDIPTERYX'S ENVIRONMENT

Caudipteryx (foreground), part of the Chinese "Gang of Three," lived in an environment like the one shown above. Forests of conifers and ginkgoes, with an undergrowth of ferns and cycads, provided refuge and food for many different animals in Late Jurassic and Early Cretaceous China. Lizards and small mammals scampered through the undergrowth, and little feathered theropod dinosaurs hunted between the trees. The air was colonized by birds (some resembling modern types), while on the ground raced several different half-dinosaur, half-bird creatures.

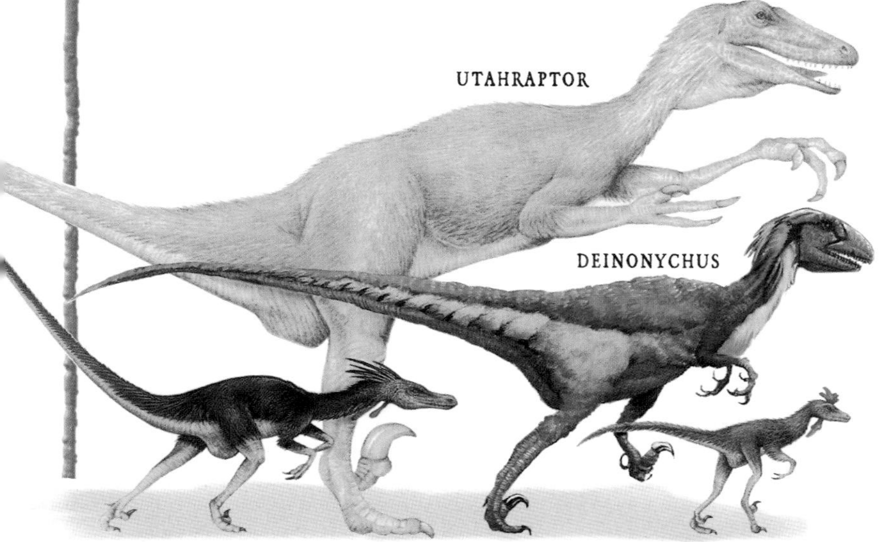

UTAHRAPTOR

DEINONYCHUS

VELOCIRAPTOR

BAMBIRAPTOR

MANIRAPTORAN DINOSAURS

The group of meat-eating dinosaurs known as the maniraptorans has always been viewed as birdlike. Attempts have been made to put them on the ancestral tree of the birds, but the problem is that, being Late Cretaceous dinosaurs, they lived much later than *Archaeopteryx*, which most scientists consider the first bird. Perhaps the maniraptorans evolved from *Archaeopteryx* or *Archaeopteryx*-like birds that lost their ability to fly. If that were true, they would have been very much like the Chinese "Gang of Three."

CHINESE "GANG OF THREE"

Across the contemporary European-Asian landmass, where China's Liaoning Province now lies, a series of forest-shrouded inland lakes produced fossils that were just as spectacular as those from Solnhofen. These include three kinds of animal that, like *Archaeopteryx*, show the evolutionary connection between birds and dinosaurs. Only recently, with improved scientific exchanges between China and the West, has their significance been fully appreciated.

SINOSAUROPTERYX

One of the little dinosaurs present in Liaoning Province was *Sinosauropteryx*. It seems to have been covered with fur or feathers. The fossil preservation is so good that a kind of downy fuzz is visible around the bones. Although there is still some dissent, most scientists are convinced that this represents a covering of "protofeathers," structures partway between hair, like that of a mammal, and feathers, like those of a bird.

SINOSAUROPTERYX FOSSIL

Only the downy covering on this skeleton shows *Sinosauropteryx* to have been related to the birds. Apart from that, it is pure meat-eating dinosaur. The long legs and tail show it to have been a swift-running animal, while the short arms displayed three claws. Three skeletons of *Sinosauropteryx* have been found, and their stomach contents show that they hunted lizards and small mammals.

HALF-BIRD, HALF-DINOSAUR

Another small animal was *Protarchaeoteryx*. It was about the same size as *Sinosauropteryx*, but it had a short tail and much longer arms. It was also covered with fuzz, and although the only skeleton found was very jumbled, there seemed to be long feathers along the arms and tail. The feathers on the arms would have given a winglike structure, but it would not have been sufficient to give the animal any power of flight.

TRIASSIC 248-206 MYA	EARLY/MID JURASSIC 206-159 MYA	LATE JURASSIC 159-144 MYA	EARLY CRETACEOUS 144-97 MYA	LATE CRETACEOUS 97-65 MYA

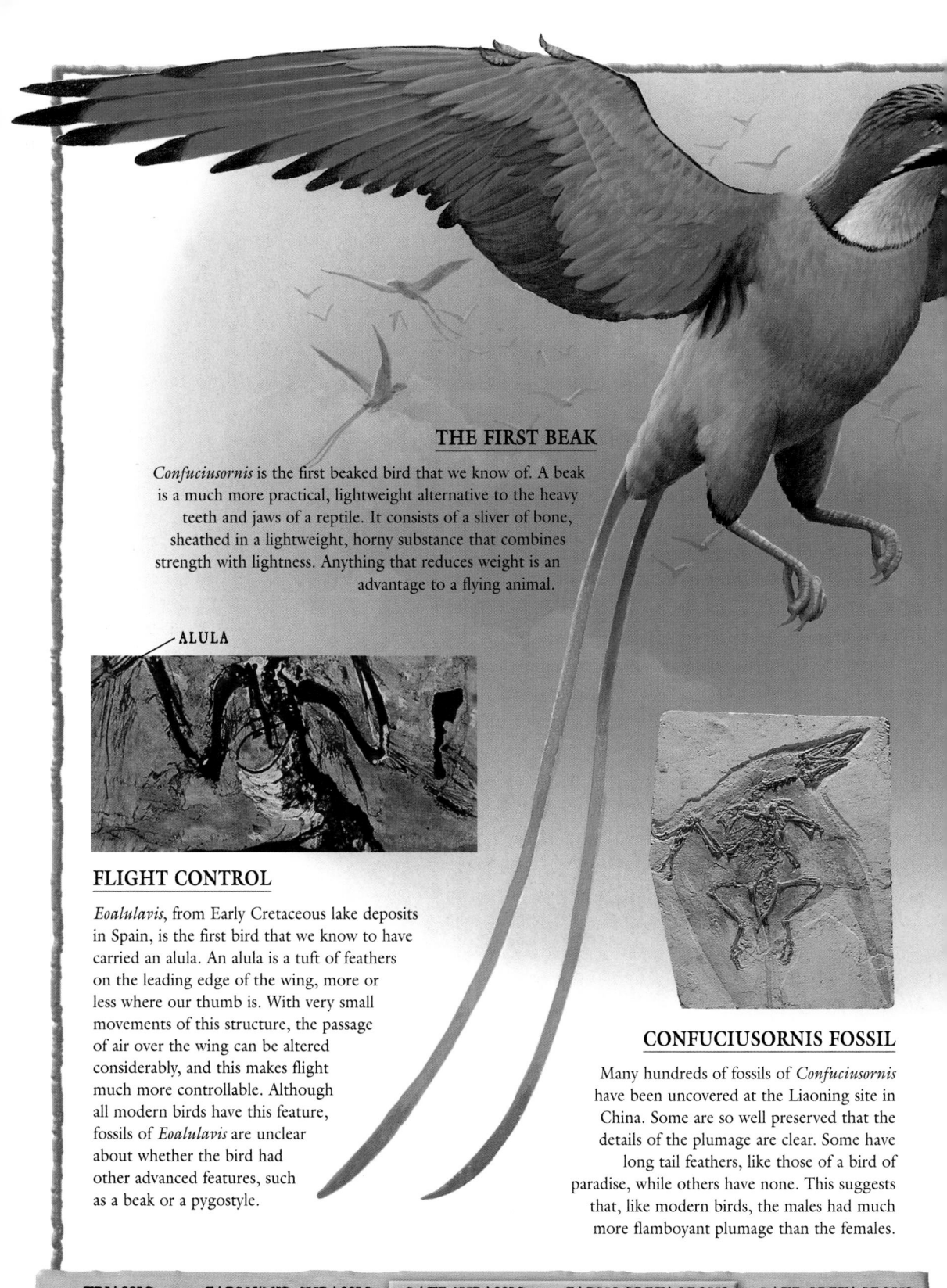

THE FIRST BEAK

Confuciusornis is the first beaked bird that we know of. A beak is a much more practical, lightweight alternative to the heavy teeth and jaws of a reptile. It consists of a sliver of bone, sheathed in a lightweight, horny substance that combines strength with lightness. Anything that reduces weight is an advantage to a flying animal.

ALULA

FLIGHT CONTROL

Eoalulavis, from Early Cretaceous lake deposits in Spain, is the first bird that we know to have carried an alula. An alula is a tuft of feathers on the leading edge of the wing, more or less where our thumb is. With very small movements of this structure, the passage of air over the wing can be altered considerably, and this makes flight much more controllable. Although all modern birds have this feature, fossils of *Eoalulavis* are unclear about whether the bird had other advanced features, such as a beak or a pygostyle.

CONFUCIUSORNIS FOSSIL

Many hundreds of fossils of *Confuciusornis* have been uncovered at the Liaoning site in China. Some are so well preserved that the details of the plumage are clear. Some have long tail feathers, like those of a bird of paradise, while others have none. This suggests that, like modern birds, the males had much more flamboyant plumage than the females.

TRIASSIC 248-206 MYA	EARLY/MID JURASSIC 206-159 MYA	LATE JURASSIC 159-144 MYA	EARLY CRETACEOUS 144-97 MYA	LATE CRETACEOUS 97-65 MYA

TOWARD MODERN BIRDS

For all its fine feathers, *Archaeopteryx* was still mostly dinosaur. It had a long reptilian tail, fingers on the wings, and a jaw full of teeth. Modern birds have stumpy tails called pygostyles supporting long feathers. Their wing fingers have completely disappeared, and they also have beaks instead of jaws and teeth. These are all weight-saving adaptations, evolved to make the bird as light as possible so that it can fly more efficiently. These features seem to have appeared at different times during the time of the dinosaurs.

A MODERN TAIL

Iberomesornis, a fossil bird from Upper Cretaceous rocks in Spain, is the earliest bird known to have a pygostyle tail. This structure consists of a muscular stump from which the tail feathers grow in a fan arrangement. The muscles of the pygostyle can spread the tail feathers out or bunch them together, helping control flight or make a display for courting purposes.

THE PERCHING FOOT

Birds that live in trees usually have feet in which the first toe is turned backward, enabling the foot to grasp a small branch so the bird can perch. An early example of a perching foot is found in *Changchengornis*, a close relative of *Confuciusornis* that is also found in the Liaoning rocks. This bird also had a hooked beak, suggesting that it was a meat eater, like a modern hawk.

HESPERORNIS BONES

Hesperornis was a swimming bird of Late Cretaceous North America. As big as a human, it must have looked something like a penguin, but with no forelimbs at all and a long beak full of teeth. This leg bone was found in chalk deposits in western Kansas.

THE DINOSAUR RE-EVOLVED?

A number of huge, flightless, hunting birds evolved around 65 million years ago, once the dinosaurs died out. *Phorusrhachos* of South America and *Diatryma* of North America were built along the lines of medium-sized meat-eating dinosaurs, with fast hind legs and fierce heads. *Titanis* (above) from Florida even had tiny clawed hands on the remains of its wings — almost as if a niche developed for dinosaur-shaped hunting creatures and evolution filled it with giant hunting birds.

KILLER DUCK

Bullockornis lived in Australia around 20 million years ago. It stood 10 feet (3 m) high and had a huge beak that was used for either cracking nuts or tearing flesh. An enlarged brain capacity suggests that the latter was more likely, since quick senses are necessary for hunting prey. *Bullockornis* was unrelated to the emus or the cassowaries or to any other type of flightless bird that exists in Australia today. Despite its dinosaur-like appearance, *Bullockornis* was actually a kind of duck.

ABANDONING FLIGHT

It seems to some scientists that often no sooner has a feature evolved than certain lines of evolution abandon it. As soon as flight evolved, some birds reverted to living on the ground. There are several explanations for this. Perhaps flightless birds evolved in areas where no dangerous predators lived on the ground, and so there was no need to fly, or perhaps food was more plentiful on the ground.

DEAD AS A DODO

Probably the best known of the extinct, flightless birds is *Raphus*, the dodo. The dodo evolved from pigeon stock into a ground-dwelling plant eater on the island of Mauritius. It survived there for thousands of years, as there were no ground-living predators. Everything changed, however, when humans arrived on the island, and the bird was wiped out within a few years.

PLANT EATERS

Not only were the shapes of the meat-eating dinosaurs reflected in some of the later birds, but bird versions of the long-necked plant eaters seem to have existed as well. *Dinorinis*, the moa, existed in New Zealand up to modern times. It thrived there because no ground-living predators lived in New Zealand — until human beings came along and wiped out the bird.

LATE CRETACEOUS 97-65 MYA	PALEOGENE 65-23 MYA	NEOGENE 23-1.8 MYA	QUATERNARY 1.8-0.01 MYA

SINCE THE DINOSAURS

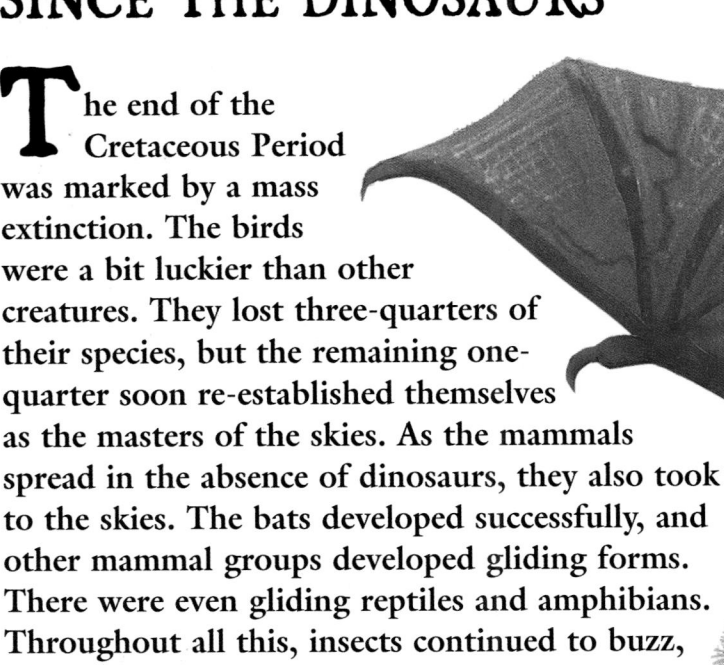

The end of the Cretaceous Period was marked by a mass extinction. The birds were a bit luckier than other creatures. They lost three-quarters of their species, but the remaining one-quarter soon re-established themselves as the masters of the skies. As the mammals spread in the absence of dinosaurs, they also took to the skies. The bats developed successfully, and other mammal groups developed gliding forms. There were even gliding reptiles and amphibians. Throughout all this, insects continued to buzz, as they have done since Carboniferous times.

THE WEBBED WAY

The birds that survived the mass extinction went on to become the true masters of the skies. Birds today mostly fly, but they can also perch, wade, swim, and even burrow. *Presbyornis* was a long-legged wading duck that lived in huge flocks in North America around 65 million years ago. Although it had webbed feet, its legs would have been too long to allow it to swim. The webs probably developed to prevent it from sinking into the mud.

THE TRUE KINGS

Insects appeared nearly 400 million years ago and immediately evolved flying types. Few died out in the mass extinction at the end of the Cretaceous, and they are now far more diverse than any other group of creatures. Wings are the tough parts of an insect's anatomy, and it is mostly wings that have been fossilized. Occasionally the preservation is so good that the patterns and markings are preserved, although the colors have long since changed.

LATE CRETACEOUS 97-65 MYA	PALEOGENE 65-23 MYA	NEOGENE 23-1.8 MYA	QUATERNARY 1.8-0.01 MYA

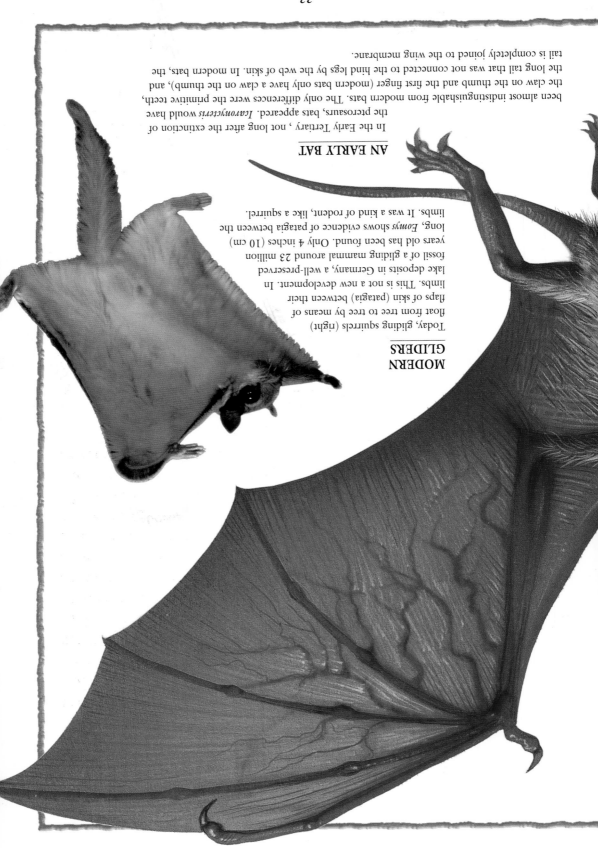

AN EARLY BAT

In the Early Tertiary , not long after the extinction of the pterosaurs, bats appeared. *Icaronycteris* would have been almost indistinguishable from modern bats. The only differences were the primitive teeth, the claw on the thumb and the first finger (modern bats only have a claw on the thumb), and the long tail that was not connected to the hind legs by the web of skin. In modern bats, the tail is completely joined to the wing membrane.

MODERN GLIDERS

Today, gliding squirrels (right) float from tree to tree by means of flaps of skin (patagia) between their limbs. This is not a new development. In lake deposits in Germany, a well-preserved fossil of a gliding mammal around 23 million years old has been found. Only 4 inches (10 cm) long, *Eomys* shows evidence of patagia between the limbs. It was a kind of rodent, like a squirrel.

DID YOU KNOW?

• There are two kinds of flight in the animal kingdom — flapping flight and gliding flight. Flapping flight requires the animal to provide all the muscular energy to produce the flying action. Gliding flight simply requires the animal to have a certain shape of wing to soar through the air.

Flapping flight is seen in birds and in pterosaurs. This kind of flight may lapse into gliding flight, when, for example, a vulture soars on rising hot air, looking for food, or an albatross skims the wave surfaces of the ocean. Watch a pigeon in flight when it is courting. It flaps its way to a particular height, then glides downward as if it on a roller coaster, and then flaps upward again. Presumably, the pterosaurs of old had similar habits, using a variety of flying techniques.

There are two types of gliding flight. In one type, the gliding action is initiated by the animal's own muscular efforts. Flying fish, for example, launch themselves into the air by swimming rapidly to the surface and using the movement of their strong tails to throw themselves out of the water. In the second type of gliding flight, the animal simply drops down from a high vantage point and, like a hang glider on a slope of air, uses its aerodynamic shape to take it where it wants to go. Flying squirrels, flying frogs, and the flying dragon lizards of Malaysia do this type of gliding to take them from a higher place to a lower place.

• Scientists disagree as to how bird flight evolved. Some say that primitive birds, such as *Archaeopteryx*, started as gliders. Others see these birds as essentially terrestrial creatures, launching themselves into the air by running quickly along the ground.

MORE BOOKS TO READ

Digging for Bird-Dinosaurs: An Expedition to Madagascar. Nic Bishop (Houghton Mifflin)

Feathered Dinosaurs. Christopher Sloan (National Geographic Society)

A Moment in Time with Sinosauropteryx. Philip J. Currie, Eva Koppelhus, and Jan Sovak (Troodon Productions)

Ornithomimus: Pursuing the Bird-Mimic Dinosaur. Monique Keiran (Raincoast Books)

Pteranodon. Discovering Dinosaurs (series). Daniel Cohen (Bridgestone Books)

Pterodactyls. Elaine Landau (Children's Press)

GLOSSARY

alula: a tuft of feathers on a bird's wing that helps the bird maintain control while in flight by influencing how air moves over the wing.

ammonites: extinct, molluslike marine animals of the Mesozoic age that had flat spiral shells.

beak: the horny, projecting bill of a bird.

chitin: the organic substance that forms the hard outer shell of insects, arachnids, and crustaceans.

crest: a projection, such as a tuft of feathers or fur, on the head of a bird or some other kind of animal.

DNA: an acid inside every living cell that carries genetic information about individual heredity.

evolution: the theory that organisms change form and develop over long periods of time, so that descendants look or behave differently than their early ancestors.

filaments: fine, thin threads of material.

fossils: remnants or impressions of organisms from a past geologic age embedded in natural materials, such as rock or resin.

glide: to fly, or soar, on air currents without natural or mechanical propulsion.

hinterland: an area or region that is inland from a coast or at a distance from cities.

lagoon: a shallow body of water, especially one separated from the sea by sandbars or coral reefs.

lithographic: capable of printing, copying, or otherwise producing an image, pattern, or impression.

magma: the molten rock material beneath Earth's crust that, when cooled, forms igneous rock.

mammals: warm-blooded, vertebrate animals, including human beings, that have hair or fur on their skin and nourish their young with milk produced in the mammary glands of the female's body.

membrane: a thin, pliable layer of tissue that covers or separates certain parts of an animal's body, such as its organs.

niche: a situation or activity well-suited to an organism's interests or abilities.

plate tectonics: the theory that Earth's continents once were a single landmass that drifted or was forced apart over billions of years.

plumage: the feathers of a bird.

pouch: a saclike structure beneath the beak of some birds for carrying food or on the abdomen of some marsupials for carrying their young.

pygostyle: the muscular, stumplike tailbone of some birds, which contains vertebrae that are fused, or joined, and which controls the movement of tail feathers.

quarries: large, open pits or excavations of land that are dug out to obtain stone, sand, or gravel.

reef: a ridge of rocks, sand, or coral at or near the surface of a body of water, usually only a short distance offshore.

reptiles: cold-blooded, egg-laying vertebrates, such as snakes, crocodiles, or turtles, that have scales or horny plates on their bodies.

sponges: primitive marine animals with porous skeletons that grow like plants and attach to surfaces underwater.

struts: bars or rods used to brace a structure against pressure along its length.

vertebrae: the segments of bone or cartilage that form an animal's spinal column.

INDEX

ACKNOWLEDGEMENTS

The original publisher would like to thank Advocate and Elizabeth Wiggans for their assistance.

Picture Credits: t=top, b=bottom, c=center, l=left, r=right
Lisa Alderson: 6b, 15b, 16-17c, 22l, 26b, 27t, 31bl. John Alston: 10l, 10-11b, 11tr, 12-13c, 13cr, 13b, 17t.
BBC Natural History Unit: 16cl. Corbis: 10t, 16b, 18c. Dr Peter Griffiths: 24t, 24b, 25r. Simon Mendez: 4-5b,
6-7c, 14-15, 15t, 18-19c, 20t, 27t, 28t, 29t, 29b, 30-31, 32l. National Museum of Wales: 9, 20b.
Natural History Museum: 5t, 8t, 12b, 14t, 18t, 23r, 31t. Paleontologisk Museum, Oslo: 6cl, 7cr, 28cr.
Luis Rey: 7b, 12tl, 19, 20-21c, 22-23, 24-25, 26t, 27bl, 30l, 32-33.

Every effort has been made to trace the copyright holders and
we apologize in advance for any unintentional errors or omissions.